So Much

"The suicide rate in the US is ⟨...⟩ ...y people don't know how to approach a friend or family member who is facing the struggle. Dr. Jantz is on a mission to save lives as he provides clear and compassionate strategies for approaching suicide intervention."

Harold G. Koenig, MD, professor of psychiatry and behavioral sciences and director of the Center for Spirituality, Theology, and Health at Duke University

"This is an impressive, uplifting book about what can be an overwhelming topic. Read it now. You need this wisdom so you can be proactive instead of reactive when (not if) someone you know doubts life is worth living. Dr. Jantz does what he says he'll do—he provides excellent help that will increase your hope. The book is easy to read and is full of inspiring illustrations, timely examples, and practical, sensible ideas and strategies. Parents, educators, pastors, and other professionals will be better prepared to love people well who live with pressures and challenges. Suicide is preventable!"

Dr. Kathy Koch, founder of Celebrate Kids, Inc.; author of *Screens and Teens*, *8 Great Smarts*, *Start with the Heart*, and *Five to Thrive*

Praise for *Healing the Scars of Addiction*

"Pain is inevitable—but misery is optional. If you are miserable because of some addiction, some repetitive pattern of behavior that only brings you suffering, then opt for freedom! In *Healing the Scars of Addiction*, Dr. Jantz has provided the tools you need to heal, to overcome—to be free!"

Timothy R. Jennings, MD, DFAPA, past president of the Tennessee and Southern Psychiatric Associations; author of *The God-Shaped Heart*

"*Healing the Scars of Addiction* provides understanding, helpful steps, and realistic hope for those who are struggling with various forms of addiction and want to reclaim their lives from addiction and move forward into a healthier life. I highly recommend it!"

Siang-Yang Tan, PhD, professor of psychology, Fuller Theological Seminary; author of *Counseling and Psychotherapy: A Christian Perspective*

Praise for *Healing the Scars of Childhood Abuse*

"*Healing the Scars of Childhood Abuse* is a very important book. It takes on the lasting implications of childhood trauma with empathy and hope. Dr. Jantz tells the story of trauma through the eyes of the children. Those stories make this book a page-turner. As the stories unfold, the author's psychological wisdom and practical insight grow organically. In this way, this book is a moving personal experience. I highly recommend this book to anyone who is ready to heal the past and build a new future."

Michael Gurian, *New York Times* bestselling author of *The Wonder of Boys* and *The Wonder of Girls*

"*Healing the Scars of Childhood Abuse* is a clearly written book that will be of great help to those dealing with the long-term effects of childhood abuse and wanting to heal and move on to deeper wholeness. I highly recommend it!"

Siang-Yang Tan, PhD, professor of psychology, Fuller Theological Seminary, and author of *Counseling and Psychotherapy: A Christian Perspective*

SO MUCH
TO
LIVE
FOR

Books by Gregory L. Jantz, PhD,
with Ann McMurray

Healing the Scars of Emotional Abuse
Overcoming Anxiety, Worry, and Fear
Every Woman's Guide to Managing Your Anger
Healing the Scars of Childhood Abuse
Healing the Scars of Addiction

Books by Gregory L. Jantz, PhD,
and Dr. Tim Clinton,
with Ann McMurray

Don't Call It Love

SO MUCH TO LIVE FOR

HOW TO PROVIDE **HELP AND HOPE** TO SOMEONE CONSIDERING SUICIDE

GREGORY L. JANTZ, PhD
WITH KEITH WALL

Revell
a division of Baker Publishing Group
Grand Rapids, Michigan

Published by Revell
a division of Baker Publishing Group
PO Box 6287, Grand Rapids, MI 49516-6287
www.revellbooks.com

Printed in the United States of America

Library of Congress Cataloging-in-Publication Data
Names: Jantz, Gregory L., author. | Wall, Keith, author.
Title: So much to live for : how to provide help and hope to someone considering suicide / Gregory L. Jantz, PhD with Keith Wall.
Description: Grand Rapids, Michigan : Revell, a division of Baker Publishing Group, [2021]
Identifiers: LCCN 2021006623 | ISBN 9780800739812 (paperback) | ISBN 9780800741310 (casebound) | ISBN 9781493431991 (ebook)
Subjects: LCSH: Suicide. | Suicide—Prevention.
Classification: LCC RC569 .J37 2021 | DDC 362.28—dc23
LC record available at https://lccn.loc.gov/2021006623

Unless otherwise indicated, Scripture quotations are from THE HOLY BIBLE, NEW INTERNATIONAL VERSION®, NIV® Copyright © 1973, 1978, 1984, 2011 by Biblica, Inc.® Used by permission. All rights reserved worldwide.

Scripture quotations labeled NASB are from the (NASB®) New American Standard Bible®, Copyright © 1960, 1971, 1977, 1995 by The Lockman Foundation. Used by permission. All rights reserved. www.lockman.org

Scripture quotations labeled NKJV are from the New King James Version®. Copyright © 1982 by Thomas Nelson. Used by permission. All rights reserved.

Published in association with The Bindery Agency, www.TheBinderyAgency.com.

The names and details of the people and situations described in this book have been changed or presented in composite form in order to ensure the privacy of those with whom the author has worked.

21 22 23 24 25 26 27   7 6 5 4 3 2 1

This book is dedicated
to all of the people who are struggling
with deep issues that lead them to think suicide
is an option to end their pain.
And to the people who love them enough
to step in and step up to make a difference.
There is indeed so much to live for.
God has guaranteed it!

Note to Readers
with a Loved One in Crisis

If you need immediate guidance on how to help someone you believe is considering self-harm, turn to:

Chapter 6: Signs and Symptoms: Red Flags That Should Put You on Red Alert

Chapter 8: Step In and Speak Up: What to Do When You Believe Someone Is Suicidal

Later, you can read the other chapters to fully understand the factors that lead someone to contemplate suicide.

Contents

Prologue

Hope amid Heartache

Future, depression, hope, and suicide.

We rarely see those words strung together as if they belong next to each other.

We know how the words *depression* and *suicide* are linked, signifying serious problems in a person's life.

And we know that *hope* and *future* fit together well, indicating the confidence to look forward with optimism.

I believe all of these words do intersect in a significant way: for people struggling with depression and related issues—even to the point of contemplating suicide—there is indeed a future and a hope. I wouldn't have written this book if I didn't believe with my whole heart that *everyone* has so much to live for.

In three decades as a mental health expert, I have counseled thousands of people who needed help coping with pain and fear of every kind: anxiety, depression, guilt, anger, addiction, and the emotional scars of physical and psychological abuse. Sometimes, my clients felt so desperate that suicide seemed like the best option—the only option—to relieve the pain.

Early in my career, I was often dismayed by the epic scope of battles people waged within themselves and the elusive struggle to achieve true healing. It seemed to me that lasting wellness and inner peace were treasures many seek but few ever find.

Then I realized something vitally important. Many of the hurting people I counseled were eager—or desperate—to overcome their troubles but lacked the key ingredient of hope. By the time these people began therapy with me or sought treatment at the clinic I founded, they had lived with their condition for so long and tried so many unfruitful treatment options that optimism had all but vanished. Distress and despair, usually caused by a variety of factors, were compounded by a fundamental lack of hopefulness and confidence that anything would ever change.

This led me to make *hope* a cornerstone of all the therapy, speaking, writing, research, and treatment planning I do. In 2014 we changed the name of our Seattle-area treatment facility after clients said, "This is a place of hope." That's exactly what we wanted and thus the name stuck; it is now called The Center: A Place of Hope. My team and I also adopted Jeremiah 29:11–14 as our clinic's guiding Scripture passage:

> "For I know the plans I have for you," declares the LORD, "plans to prosper you and not to harm you, plans to give you hope and a future. Then you will call on me and come and pray to me, and I will listen to you. You will seek me and find me when you seek me with all your heart. I will be found by you," declares the LORD, "and will bring you back to the place from which I carried you into exile."

I encourage all of my clients and those who read my books—including you—to reflect on these life-changing words and embrace them as a touchstone in the pursuit of emotional, spiritual, and physical wellness. After all, persistently depressed and troubled people often feel that they are in captivity of sorts—trapped and immobilized by a force bigger than themselves. But God is eager and able to set them free. No matter how much pain someone is currently experiencing—no matter how despairing and anguished—there is hope that the troubled person can regain health, recapture joy, restore balance, and reclaim optimism.

I assure you this is not a simplistic perspective on a complex issue. I have provided psychological treatment for thousands of struggling clients, I have conducted extensive research on the topic of suicide, and now I have written this volume on suicide prevention. I take a clear-eyed view of this troubling topic, especially during the troubling times in which we live.

I say with both realism and optimism that hope can prevail over dark circumstances and belief in the future can provide the inspiration to press on. I have seen scores of people meet their worries, fear, and anxieties head-on, helping them break through to recovery. I've seen the amazing courage of those who refused to cower any longer in a corner of their lives and reached out and up to personal victory. I've seen hope win out over despair, trust win out over fear, faith triumph over adversity.

Since you have picked up this book, it's likely there is someone you are deeply concerned about. And you have reason to be concerned. According to Mental Health America, more than 10.3 million US adults have had serious suicidal thoughts.[1] Complicating matters, more than 10 million adults have an unmet need for mental health treatment.[2] The World Health Organization estimates 800,000 people take their lives each year—one every forty seconds.[3] This is an issue we cannot turn a blind eye to, and we should feel compelled to reach out in love to those whose behaviors cause us alarm. Thank you for your willingness to step in and make a difference in the life of someone you know.

Before we move on, I want to tell you four points that guide my thinking and writing on this subject:

Having concerns about a loved one's possible suicide is one of the most fearful, alarming, and stressful situations you can find yourself in. But I firmly believe there is always hope, no matter how desperate the circumstances seem. It's also important that you, as a concerned loved one, take care of yourself in the midst of crisis, attending to your health in every way so you can remain strong and wise.

Family, friends, and close caregivers are often the first to recognize the warning signs of suicide and can be the first to step in to help an at-risk individual. In the pages ahead, we'll look closely at the signs and symptoms of a suicidal individual, the vital role of loved ones in intervening, and the most effective ways you can assist the struggling person in your life. You are in a vital position to provide hope and help when it's needed most.

You can be instrumental in helping to save the life of the suicidal person in your life. Your preparation, compassion, and proactive intervention can literally make a difference between life and death. I hasten to add something else crucially important here (and will reiterate later): Although you can be extremely influential, offering true hope and help, you are not responsible for another person's choices. You can only do your part, with the expectation that your friend or family member will find the strength to pursue health.

God cares deeply about hurting people, and he wants all to experience the fullness and joyfulness of life that he intended. As we read in Scripture, "The LORD is close to the brokenhearted and saves those who are crushed in spirit" (Ps. 34:18). He heals wounds and repairs brokenness. He can use significant individuals—including you—to help those who feel desperate and distraught. What's more, the Great Physician often brings healing through the expertise of human physicians and mental health practitioners. That's why people with loved ones suffering from a mental issue need to reach out to professional counselors as soon as possible.

The person you care about can find healing and wholeness—and go on to experience hope in a better future. Though *depression* and *suicide* are daunting words, *future* and *hope* contain far more power—power to mend what is broken and restore lost joy.

PART 1

UNDERSTANDING YOUR LOVED ONE'S DESPERATE STRUGGLE

—1—

Lifelines

The Vital Role of Family, Friends, and Close Caregivers

Legendary newspaper columnist Walter Winchell has been credited with observing, "A real friend is one who walks in when the rest of the world walks out."

As a concerned friend or family member, you're reading this book because you care deeply about an individual who is struggling intensely, who is somewhere in the downward spiral that could result in attempted suicide. You want to help, to do what you can to stop the torment your loved one is wrestling against, to help them find peace. You're the kind of person Winchell was talking about: when your friend feels friendless, you've demonstrated the courage and love to walk toward them, embrace them, and bolster them amid the battle.

I sincerely commend you for being that friend your loved one needs right now. It's a tough role, I know. "There is no physician like a true friend," goes the classic saying, and you are being a true friend in a very difficult situation. Thank you for your courage and care.

What You Uniquely Offer

To the troubled person, a caring family member or concerned friend like you is likely in the best position to help because a relationship has already been established. You know them, they know you, and you've built at least a foundational level of camaraderie and communication. You have earned their trust, and they may be more willing to share their thoughts with you than with other acquaintances. Now they need your eye contact—both literally and emotionally. They need to know that they are valued in your sight.

You care enough to educate yourself about the descent into darkness and what you can do to help them break free. This knowledge, and your foreknowledge of their personality, can enable you to detect temperament changes and danger signs more readily than a casual acquaintance could.

As an informed friend or family member, you're more likely to know or suspect the issues that fuel their suicidal ideation. Through observation or interaction, you now may be about to detect the discouragement, diminishment, and depression they have internalized—and their difficulty letting go and moving on.

And because of previously established trust and friendship, they are more likely to listen when you speak. You've earned the right and trust to speak into their distress. Whether you speak gentle encouragement or tough love, they need you to be straightforward as long as you do so with gentle respect. This is something a caring friend or family member can offer more authentically than a mere acquaintance can.

Proverbs 18:24 tells us that "there is a friend who sticks closer than a brother," meaning that a true friend cares so much that they won't give up no matter how tough things get. They will be there for you even when things get ugly. Thank you for being that kind of friend to your troubled loved one.

But I must also share some important words of caution—because I care about *you* as much as I care about your friend.

Beware of Caregiver Stress and Possible Codependency

The truth is, many loving, well-intentioned people take on too much responsibility for their troubled individual. They experience feelings of frustration, anger, awkwardness, fear, and exhaustion. They may even blame themselves and play the self-condemning "if only" game: *If only I had supported him more . . . If only I hadn't said what I said . . . If only. . . .*

So here are my honest words of truth to you: Please keep in mind that you didn't cause your loved one's condition. You can't control it and you can't cure it. Their condition is the result of their choices, not yours.

Yes, you love them. And you absolutely, positively care about helping them from the deadly descent. But please know that people make their own choices, and your loved one is making theirs. You can encourage, but you cannot determine their mental and emotional well-being. You place an unfair, unimaginable burden upon yourself if you believe it's up to you to keep another person from committing suicide. You may become so preoccupied with watching and helping them that your own health and well-being suffer from the strain.[1]

I invite you to take a moment for an honest self-assessment.

Assess Yourself

Are you experiencing some of the common signs of caregiver stress? The Mayo Clinic has suggested several to watch for:

- Feeling overwhelmed or constantly worried
- Feeling tired often
- Getting too little or too much sleep
- Gaining or losing weight
- Becoming easily irritated or angry
- Losing interest in activities you once enjoyed
- Feeling sad

- Having frequent headaches or other physical ailments
- Feeling depressed and/or anxious[2]

To that list I'll add feelings of fear, embarrassment, or hopelessness. Did you identify with one or more of those symptoms? You may be feeling the stress more than you realized. And if your own strength is depleted and your reserves spent, you'll have little strength from which to encourage and help a loved one in need.

Dealing with a potentially suicidal friend can so preoccupy your time, thoughts, and energy that you allow yourself to be drained of the pleasures that used to bring you joy. I strongly urge you to make the time to keep yourself strong—physically, mentally, emotionally, and spiritually.

In their book *Beyond Addiction: How Science and Kindness Help People Change*, the authors explain the importance and benefit of taking care of yourself as you care for another:

> How can you accept your loved one until she stops what she is doing? One way is to have your well-being not wholly depend on her, and by devoting energy to something outside of your concerns for her. When you take care of yourself, you build strength to both tolerate what you can't change and change what you can. At the same time, as a calmer, happier person, you will be contributing to an atmosphere that is conducive to the change you hope to see in your loved one, and you will be modeling healthy behaviors you wish for in your loved one.[3]

Note especially the statement, "When you take care of yourself, you build strength to both tolerate what you can't change and change what you can." It's like the pitch the flight attendant gives as you're buckling up in an airplane: "Put on your own oxygen mask first, then help the child next to you with theirs." The reason is that it's far easier to help a struggling person if you're not

Simon Says, "Stay Steady and Strong"

Simon recalls his close friend's emotional battle like it was yesterday. In reality, it was nearly twelve years ago, when Simon and Beth were seniors in college. Through their high school years they had enjoyed a friendship—always just friends—sharing everything about their lives with each other.

"Beth was a wonderful, thoughtful person, but she struggled with big mood swings," Simon remembers. "She was introspective, sensitive, and artistic. I always knew when she was feeling down, but usually I didn't know exactly why."

Once Beth called Simon late at night after a date, euphoric that her boyfriend had proposed marriage. But soon the romance was dampened by frequent blowups, and four months into the engagement, in the final semester of their senior year, Beth's fiancé broke it off. "You're too high-maintenance for me," he told her.

Beth was devastated. The weeks that followed were consumed by tears, withdrawal, skipped classes, and self-loathing. She disappeared from Simon's life for weeks at a time, despite his frequent attempts to stay in contact. Eventually, she resurfaced and reengaged with Simon, pouring out her heart and hurt.

Simon reflects on those days: "As Beth's friend, I did everything I could think of to try to help her. We stayed up late to talk and cry. I told her the guy didn't deserve her. I tried to get her to go out with friends. But Beth just wanted to stay home, closed off from the world.

"Once, when talking on the phone," Simon recalls, "Beth mumbled something I couldn't quite hear. I asked her to repeat it and she said, only slightly louder, 'I'm not worth this.'"

Beth's depression soon slid into despair. "You all would be better off without me," she said more than once. Simon then became really worried. He would lie awake at night, fearing that his troubled friend would attempt to harm herself. He did everything he could think of to help Beth. Looking back, Simon admits he often grew frustrated that his friend wouldn't take care of herself and couldn't "pull herself out of" those dark places.

The breakthrough came when Simon finally talked with a psychology professor, who strongly recommended helping Beth get mental-health guidance from a qualified professional. He gave Simon a referral, and Simon convinced his friend to set the appointment. Actually, this step became a double breakthrough, because the therapist immediately recognized that Beth needed a significant intervention since she had been teetering on suicidal ideation for a long time. And Simon realized that he had become enmeshed in this unhealthy relationship. While trying to help his friend, Simon had become emotionally and physically drained.

Beth received the preventive help she so desperately needed. Her work lasted the rest of the semester, and she continued therapy for two more years after graduation.

Simon, too, got much-needed insight through counseling. It took only a few therapy sessions for him to learn that, ultimately, Beth's life choices were not his responsibility. Though his care for Beth was commendable and genuinely loving, he learned that he couldn't continue to invest so heavily at his own expense. Simon learned to take care of himself, to preserve his own strength, and to invest in his friend's health only when it would not compromise his own health.

"I almost let Beth's troubles become my troubles," Simon says today. "I know now that it's not unloving to step back a bit, to not invest so emotionally in a friend's trauma. You can't be much help if you're a mess yourself. You've got to stay steady and strong."

After all these years, Simon and Beth remain friends, now both in happy marriages of their own and enjoying fulfilling work. With the perspective of time and space, Simon reflects on the experience of years ago: "When a friend or family member is struggling deeply, of course you want to step in to help. That's what it means to love someone. In the process, you have to love yourself enough to protect your own health and not get completely dragged into the other person's pain. You can only offer help to others if you are helping yourself all along the way."

struggling for air yourself. If you first take care of yourself, you'll stay stronger, calmer, and better able to encourage and help your struggling loved one.

Take Care of Yourself Too

Resolve not to let your loved one's battle rob you of your own life or your own joy. Keeping yourself strong will enable you to stay strong for them and still live life on your own terms. If you're not already doing so, eat nourishing meals and snacks. Be sure you're hydrating with plenty of water throughout the day. Take a good multivitamin and mineral supplement with a healthy meal. Avoid the jitters by limiting your coffee consumption to just one or two cups in the morning.

Get plenty of outdoor exercise: walk, run, bike, hike outdoors at least twenty to thirty minutes each day, breathing deeply and enjoying the sun's natural vitamin D. Inside or outside, add some weight-bearing exercises such as push-ups, crunches, squats, and bicep curls to keep your muscles toned.

Even better: encourage your friend to exercise regularly with you. Seeking their companionship will show them that you value their company and that you care. And the heart-pumping exercise will release wonderful endorphins into their system, which reduce any physical pain and also flood the system with temporary feelings of pleasure, satisfaction, and well-being.

Frankly, on some days you may feel so weary that self-care is the last thing you want to think about. But down times like these are when you need to make time for yourself the most and when exercise will do you the most good. Give it just a few minutes and you'll quickly see what I mean.

A friend of mine makes prayer times of her daily walks. As the exertion and deep breathing calm and refresh her body, her prayer walks with God calm and refresh her mind and spirit. He cares, and he doesn't want you to bear this burden alone.

Reclaim Your Joy

During these difficult times, take the initiative to reclaim activities that nourish your soul. Helping your loved one does not mean giving up your own life. A big part of healthy self-care is keeping your own life going—continuing those activities that invigorate you and bring a smile to your heart.

What are at least five activities that bring you pleasure and joy? Going to a movie? Lunch with friends? It could be a massage, a manicure or pedicure, a hike in the hills, a day at the zoo. Morning quiet times with God, your Bible, and a good cup of coffee. Planting and tending a garden. Turning on some upbeat music and singing like no one's listening or dancing like no one's watching.

Don't think it's selfish to attend to your own needs when someone else is suffering. Reclaiming your joy is not selfish; it is vital to your well-being and to your caregiving. Keep living your life. Nourish your body and soul. Do what brings you joy. You will be stronger because of it—and a better friend for your loved one.

You Are Not Alone

You are not alone in this. All around you is an array of people who are going through what you're facing—and studies have shown that social support can help you build resilience against stress and provide you with practical ideas for dealing with your loved one.

Don't hesitate to reach out to a qualified counselor for help and advice. They can also refer you to relevant support groups that enable caregivers to voice their concerns and encourage one another. Both individual counseling and group support can give you healthy outlets to process your emotions and equip you for the challenges you're facing.

Most importantly, keep in mind that assisting your struggling friend does not—and *should not*—stop with you. As we've stated early and often, the sooner you can get your loved one to a medical

26

or mental health professional, the better. Through apt and timely medication and counseling, they can take your friend's care above and beyond what you're able to do.

You Are the Difference

Meanwhile, please do carry on with your vital role of helper and encourager. First take good care of yourself. While you are not ultimately responsible for your friend's choices, you will be further enabled to love, intervene, and make a positive difference by being a true friend.

—2—

Why Here, Why Now?

Factors Fueling the Modern-Day Suicide Surge

"Why on earth would anyone want to die? I mean, life is *good*, right?"

Those frantic words poured out of Marv's mouth the moment he sat down in my office. But his anguished expression made it clear he was desperate for me to confirm what he said, as if a previously invincible belief was suddenly under siege.

Just twenty-four hours earlier, Marv had endured every parent's nightmare, when a knock at the door turned out to be a police officer with unwelcome news. No, there had not been a car accident, the uniformed woman quickly assured him. Still, she was there to inform Marv that his son, Jason, was in critical condition at a nearby hospital.

"Was he attacked?" Marv asked in alarm, imagining a mugging or assault.

"Sir, I'm sorry to inform you that your son appears to have tried to end his own life," she said.

As Marv recounted the experience to me, he said, "It was like she was suddenly speaking a foreign language. I couldn't get her words to make any sense."

Marv is a good example of how lots of us view suicide—as something so foreign and outside our direct experience as to be practically incomprehensible. "Why?" we demand to know, as if any answer to that question can be nothing but absurd.

In time, I began to counsel Jason on his journey to recovery. I assure you, *he* had answers to that question that were, to him, anything but absurd. Even after he was able to see that killing himself was not a proper solution to the issues he faced, those problems remained real—a clear and present obstacle to living a happy, healthy life.

In one respect, Marv's confusion could be understood. Jason had earned a master of business administration degree at age twenty-three and gone straight to work for a respectable and prosperous financial planning firm. He bought a nice house at twenty-six and drove a car that cost several times what Marv paid for his first modest house—after years of saving. Jason always seemed to be dating someone new but never got serious about anyone. He traveled to exotic destinations. He bought his dad expensive toys.

By all the usual measurements, Jason's life was good.

Except that it wasn't.

Beneath the shiny surface, Jason had a serious addiction problem—to drugs, mostly cocaine, and to frequent sex. Both dependencies had started to negatively affect his professional performance and his future at the company. To top that off, much of the money he spread around had come from the day trading he did "on the side." But he'd recently gotten burned on a couple of deals and was suddenly upside down with no way out that he could see.

No way out.

No hope left.

No one to turn to.

30

This is how Jason described the thoughts that prompted his decision to end his life. Sadly, there is nothing unique in any of those emotions. Pick any suicide story and you'll find someone who reached these same conclusions, no matter how different their personal challenges were.

A Hard Truth

The sad fact is that people like Jason—who come to believe they have more reasons to die than to go on living—do not arrive there in a vacuum. They are not simply flawed or broken individuals whose decision to commit suicide can be dismissed as a mysterious personal failure. There is no gender, age group, profession, social stratum, or income level that is immune to suicide. And the worst news is, this tragic outcome is on the rise.

According to data gathered by the Centers for Disease Control and Prevention (CDC), between 1999 and 2019, suicide rates increased in nearly every state—and by at least 30 percent in more than half of them. Averaged together, the national rate of increase approached 35 percent during that time. Consider these numbers:

- In 2019 alone, more than 47,500 people killed themselves.
- In the United States suicide is the second leading cause of death among people ages 10–34, the fourth leading cause among people ages 35–44, and the fifth leading cause among people ages 45–54.
- One person dies by suicide in our country every eleven minutes.
- In 2019, 12 million adults seriously considered suicide, 3.5 million made a plan, and 1.4 million made an attempt.
- More than half (54 percent) of people who committed suicide did not have a known mental health disorder.[1]

That last point is worth giving special attention. It serves to upend a stereotype that most people hold about suicide. It's commonly believed that trying to end one's own life is always associated with some other mental health issue—that the impulse to commit suicide is a *result* of some other mental condition.

Not so, say the numbers. Anyone can suddenly find themselves in circumstances that lead them to conclude—as Jason did—that there is no other way.

That brings us back to the question we started with: *Why?*

Think again about Marv's assertion that "life is good." That phrase perfectly captures the attitude we all grow up believing. You'll see it everywhere—on T-shirts, coffee mugs, bumper stickers. It's the subliminal message conveyed in the music playing in shopping malls and grocery stores. Some songs say it directly—"Don't worry, be happy." It's catchy, and we want to believe it.

But is it true? Certainly, it is possible to find good in nearly every circumstance or event. Sages and mystics have encouraged us for millennia to find joy in the present, no matter what happens. However, that's a coping strategy, not proof that life is *always* good, that no one should ever despair or lose hope.

No, that interpretation is not true. In fact, it is *increasingly* untrue. The hard reality is that, while tough times have always existed for individuals and nations, we now live in a particularly difficult moment in history. This has been the case for some time, but since the COVID-19 pandemic, it has become much harder to deny. Rising rates of suicide—even among the very young—are not some sociological mystery or anomaly. It is happening more often now because in some key ways our society is in *distress*.

A Perfect Storm

When people come to The Center for help with a wide range of mental health concerns, we've learned to expect that they are not struggling with a single stressor in their lives but an entire basket

SURVIVORS SPEAK:
Marissa's Bright Future and Dark Descent

"Marissa was the kind of kid who organized the kickball games on the playground in second grade," said Kirsten, Marissa's older sibling. "She was elected to the student council her freshman year of high school and was president the next year."

Kirsten was speaking at a support group for people who had survived the loss of a loved one to suicide. It had been one month since her sister killed herself with an overdose of prescription painkillers.

"She really cared about things, you know? Carried them, like she was somehow personally responsible for whether kids had enough time to eat lunch when the school went on a new schedule."

After high school, Marissa studied political science and prelaw in college. She joined several activist groups pushing for urgent action on climate change, animal rights, racial inequality, and human trafficking. She joined the staff of a student-run newspaper that ran stories drawing attention to the plight of everything from honeybees to child laborers in Africa. She campaigned relentlessly at every level of politics for candidates she believed in.

"We were all sure she was destined to run the world someday," said Kirsten.

Then a change came over Marissa. Overnight, she became withdrawn and moody. She missed meetings and slept long hours. She elected to stay at school over the holidays that fall and was slow to return family phone calls.

"I was concerned," Kirsten said, "but thought she had just finally hit a wall and needed to take a break. When we did talk, she assured me she was okay."

But she wasn't. Two things had happened to cause her view of the world to unravel. First, she was sexually assaulted by a fellow activist—a young man from a wealthy and influential family. The shame of that—and the incongruity of his actions compared to his public persona in their circle of friends—were a profound shock to her confidence.

After all her years of fighting for causes, this was one she couldn't face, so she said nothing. Then, she discovered that a local minister was skimming money from a fund set up to benefit victims of Hurricane Maria in Puerto Rico. What hope was there, she wrote in a journal, when people could be so cruel and selfish?

"I think she kept all this to herself because to share it would have cast doubt on the thing she'd built her life on—the belief that if we work hard enough the world could be a much better place," Kirsten shared. "She just lost faith—in everything."

Kirsten concluded her testimony that evening with a heartfelt plea: "If you know someone who cares deeply about fixing what's wrong with the world, please watch for signs that the weight of that is becoming too much. Don't let them be crushed because they were carrying it alone. I now wish I had seen the signs that Marissa was spiraling downward. Sometimes people who seem to have it all together are struggling just as much as or more than those with obvious troubles."

of them. In all my books—this one included—I describe what I call the "whole-person approach" to healing. This idea posits that there is no single treatment or technique that can be applied like the wave of a magic wand to make problems disappear. Healing is a broad-spectrum activity that involves every aspect of a person's mental, physical, and spiritual nature and lifestyle.

The growing problem of suicide provides the perfect opportunity to shed light on the reciprocal truth—that the kind of pain and despair that causes someone to contemplate ending their life typically also comes from a number of different directions at once. That's why, after a suicide attempt, a person often feels at a loss to pinpoint precisely why they made the choice they did. I believe it's because the five major areas of modern life listed below are more than the sum of parts but combine to form a pervasive *atmosphere* of distress. Let's look at each broad category separately.

Civil Distress

It seems that each presidential election (and even statewide and local contests) is referred to by commentators as "the most contentious ever." Few people would disagree that recent elections have indeed been incredibly contentious and combative. We are intensely divided on a number of fronts—economics, education, health care, foreign policy, and environmental protection, to name just a few. However, disagreement on important issues is to be expected in any healthy democratic society.

What makes our current political atmosphere stressful is the extreme level of vitriol between even the elected officials of opposing parties. Not only has discourse become increasingly divisive, but in many cases it also has ceased to exist entirely in any constructive form. Conversation has been overrun by increasingly strident confrontation.

To make matters worse, at a time when we desperately need reliable information from which to form cogent opinions, the national news media appear to have succumbed to this atmosphere of unrest—by choosing sides and seeming to skew their reporting in support of partisan agendas. That only serves to erode our ability to trust important institutions to serve the truth rather than self-interest.

In this environment, then, people who feel strongly about advancing a cause they are passionate about can sometimes conclude, *There's no way out. No hope left. Nowhere to turn.* Some—perhaps like those who have recently expressed their frustration by rioting and looting in a number of large cities—turn to overt violence and hostility as an outlet. Others direct their distress inward in self-destructive behavior. A few of those may even choose violence against themselves as a solution to their fear and pain.

Economic Distress

If you watch television commercials, you could easily get the idea that everyone has lots of disposable money to spend—on cars, jewelry, and exotic vacations. While that may be true for some people, their numbers have been steadily shrinking in recent decades. According to the Pew Research Center, "the wealth gap between America's richest and poorer families more than doubled between 1989 and 2016." (Wealth is defined as the value of assets a family owns, such as homes, investments, or savings accounts, minus debt, like mortgages and student loans.) According to experts at the Pew Research Center:

In 1989, the richest 5 percent of families had 114 times as much wealth as families in the second quintile (one tier above the lowest), at the median $2.3 million compared with $20,300. By 2016, the top 5 percent held 248 times as much wealth at the median. (The median wealth of the poorest 20 percent is either zero or negative in most years we examined.) [2]

Debt plays a large role in numbers like that. According to Debt.org, combined household debt in America reached a record $13.21 trillion in 2018. The share of that load carried by the average household is now $137,063—compared to $50,971 in 2000. In 1989 only 8.9 percent of households had student loan debt, at an average of around $5,400 each. In 2016 that rate climbed to 22.4 percent and an average debt of $34,200. [3]

In other words, today the vast majority of Americans are much more likely to struggle with economic insecurity than people did just thirty years ago. To be clear, for most of them, that is not about whether or not they take a family vacation this year—but about affording more fundamental things such as rent, food, car repairs, or health care. For many, the constant worry and stress take a heavy mental and emotional toll.

Social Distress

Something has gone wrong with how we relate to one another and how we communicate. We've already discussed the impact of this in our politics, where public discourse is increasingly combative and divisive. But the same condition has crept into our personal relationships as well—and many believe this is largely due to online social media and news sites. Journalism and digital discourse scholar Marie K. Shanahan wrote in 2016, "Civility took leave of open discussions years ago—online. Beneath digital news stories and social media posts are unmoderated, often anonymous comment streams showing in plain view the anger, condescension, misogyny, xenophobia, racism and nativism simmering within the citizenry."[4]

More research is needed to sort out whether so much online hatefulness is caused by the content of those sites or if they simply reveal a troubling state of the human heart. Either way, we are increasingly exposed to—and engaged in—toxic and aggressive speech via comment features online. This is one factor that led me to write a short volume called *Social Media and Depression*, which links poor mental health outcomes with unhealthy use of multiple digital platforms. In it I discuss the dangers identified by researchers, which include:

- Increased anxiety and depression
- Distorted sense of identity
- Connection addiction and FOMO—the fear of missing out
- Lower self-esteem and comparison anxiety
- A false sense of intimacy
- Cyberbullying
- Physical stagnation
- Decreased happiness and satisfaction in life[5]

Take note of the last item in the context of our current topic—the staggering increase in suicide rates in the United States. If less happiness and satisfaction is the result for some people of daily exposure to online media, then it's not far-fetched to say they could be less resilient when major problems arise in their lives.

Health Distress

Another item on the bulleted list above—physical stagnation—carries its own set of harmful consequences. Coupled with poor diet and little or no exercise, it leads to a number of chronic conditions. One of the easiest of those to assess is the number of people who are obese. According to the CDC, in 2016, 39.8 percent of American adults met the criteria for that diagnosis—a body mass index of 30 or higher. If you include those who are classified as "overweight" (with BMI between 25 and 30), the rate climbs to 71.6 percent.[6] Associated conditions include diabetes, high blood pressure, heart disease and strokes, certain types of cancer, and kidney disease.[7]

Dealing with poor health—no matter its source—is a stressful and draining experience. But that is compounded by another chronic condition in many societies—poor *access* to adequate care. According to the US Census, in 2018, 27.5 million people lacked health insurance in America—or 8.5 percent of the population. But that number doesn't tell the whole story. Thinking back to our earlier discussion of economic distress, some of those people are covered by plans with high deductibles that prohibit someone with limited income from taking full advantage of available health care.

The combination of chronic poor health and financial strain are, for many people, a perfect storm of hopelessness and despair.

Spiritual Distress

In recent decades, religious leaders have struggled to understand, much less reverse, a stark trend—the sharp decline in church membership and changes in attitudes regarding religion in general.

Between 2000 and 2019, the percentage of American adults who claim to have no religious affiliation has more than doubled, from 8 percent to 19 percent. During that same period, the number of people who claimed membership in a church, synagogue, or mosque fell from 70 percent to 50 percent.[8]

Journalist Mel Walker describes the situation this way:

> Religion is becoming increasingly irrelevant in today's Western culture. There was once a time when Christianity dominated American society. Regular attendance and participation in the church was a priority and a benefit, and most of this country's citizens looked at life from a Christian perspective. That is no longer the case. It seems as if the majority of people no longer accept a Christian worldview.[9]

One consequence is that many people no longer have access to the kind of internal spiritual resources and external support that belonging to a faith community affords in a crisis.

The Road to Recovery

I recognize that I've painted a rather bleak picture of American society in this chapter. Yet I repeat what I said earlier: the increase in suicide rates today has not happened in a vacuum, and there is nothing to be gained if we are unable to be honest with ourselves about that. The sooner we bravely assess our current atmosphere of distress and the reasons for it, the quicker we'll find our way back out again. And, as we'll see in the next chapter, these specific areas of distress have direct bearing on the most common reasons people give for considering or attempting suicide.

I'm most eager for you to keep reading and discover the heart of my message—that for all our troubles, hope is ever present. These are trends, and trends can be reversed—including the rising incidence of suicide. As Paul wrote in Ephesians 3:20, that's because we look to God for help, "who is able to do immeasurably more than all we ask or imagine, according to his power that is at work within us."

—3—

Why They Do It

Common Causes of Suicide

Trying to nail down the reason why a person chooses to take their own life is like asking what caused World War II and expecting a single, simple answer. In truth, suicide is usually the result of multiple factors and influences that reinforce and aggravate one another until it's virtually impossible to separate them. Furthermore, often the victim takes those answers with them, leaving us with a mystery we may never solve.

Still, it's worth the effort to try, because understanding the most common circumstances that prompt thoughts of suicide can help us intervene *before* it takes root in a troubled heart. That is, anything we do to make life a little easier for everyone counts as suicide prevention. This chapter helps us to focus our effort on those challenges that are known to contribute to suicidal impulses in people who are suffering.

A Common Thread

In a moment we'll examine specific circumstances and events that statistics suggest are the most typical causes of suicidal behavior.

But first, let's consider the more general emotional conditions that all of those things have in common. These four items describe the state of mind that develops as a *result* of particular stressors and triggers—which is what sets the person who becomes suicidal apart from someone in similar circumstances who finds the resiliency needed to overcome. These include:

Hopelessness. A person who is at risk of self-harm as a result of some crisis has concluded that there is no way their circumstances will ever improve—that everything good about the life they had known is gone forever, beyond salvaging. Worse, whatever pushed them to that misguided belief has poisoned their future as well. No past to return to + no future to look forward to = *no hope.*

Feeling trapped. The next stage in the downward progression is to decide there is absolutely nothing that can be done about the hopeless condition of their life. A lot has been said about the basic human instinct to either fight or flee in the face of danger. The person contemplating suicide believes they are truly cornered—in checkmate—and can do neither.

Isolation. The other primal impulse in such dire straits is to call for help. But it's not unusual for the person who has lost hope because of the crisis they face, and who feels unable to escape it, to conclude that help isn't available because no one understands their particular predicament. Solutions don't exist, because no one else has faced the same thing. Cutting themselves off like this reinforces their hopelessness and the sensation of being trapped. But it also adds a new dimension: the horrible belief that they are completely *alone* and that the present pain will *never end.*

Despair. Up until now, much of this progression takes place in the rational mind. It's a painful calculus but is still rooted in logic: *this* is true, therefore *that* must also be true, and so on. Despair, by contrast, is what all of that *feels* like. It is the cold emptiness that settles in a person's heart—and is very hard to dislodge once it does.

Keep these four stages in mind as we look more closely at specific kinds of stressors. Here's why: It is too simplistic to say that a person committed suicide because of a financial crisis or trouble with a relationship or a problem with substance abuse. Those things are all pathways that lead to the real source of trouble—hopelessness, feeling trapped, isolation, and despair.

Mixed Motives

I promised in the last chapter that many of the signs of cultural distress we discussed would have direct bearing on the reasons why people choose to die by suicide or to make an attempt on their lives. It's time to back that up with some data. Through all of 2015, the known or probable reasons for suicide were identified by coroners and law enforcement officials in twenty-seven states—and collected by the CDC's National Violent Death Reporting System. You'll notice that some important categories are missing, of course. We'll get to those in a moment. But even in short, these numbers are informative for a couple of key reasons, as we'll see.

Of the deaths by suicide covered in the study, the reasons were pinpointed as follows:

- Relationship problems (42 percent)
- Crisis in the past or upcoming two weeks (29 percent)
- Problematic substance use (28 percent)
- Physical health problem (22 percent)
- Financial/employment problems (16 percent)
- Criminal legal problems (9 percent)
- Loss of housing (4 percent)[1]

First, notice how these reasons reinforce the idea that we've got a suicide problem in America because we've got a societal health and well-being problem. Clearly, many of these people were struggling with some of the trying life difficulties we identified in the last chapter.

Second, notice how many of these categories are certain to aggravate and inflame each other—underscoring my emphasis on taking a whole-person approach to treatment. The kind of despair that leads to suicide has no single cause and no single cure. For instance, a person's relationships are almost certain to be strained by everything else on the list—financial trouble, criminal problems, and so forth. Financial strain can lead to loss of housing or to an increase in substance use as a means of self-medication. One or more of these pressures in combination could indeed provoke an acute crisis—cited as the reason for suicide in 29 percent of cases studied.

The point should be clear by now: a person's motives for suicide are anything but simple.

Tragic Factors

With that in mind, here are four categories of reasons why people commit suicide.

Mental Disorders

In the last chapter I shared CDC data suggesting that more than half (54 percent) of suicide victims have no known existing mental health disorder. That is an important point to grasp in order to challenge stereotypes and realize that anyone can be at risk of suicidal behavior, given the right circumstances. Now it's time to consider the other half of that statistic—the estimated 46 percent who *do* have a known preexisting mental disorder. In fact, that number is probably much higher when you consider that underlying disorders may indeed exist without being officially diagnosed.

In particular, here are four that are known to increase risk of suicide in some people:

Depression. This is, by far, the disorder most commonly associated with suicide. A 2018 Australian study investigated the link between depression and suicide. Of 1,051 participants, 364 reported a lifelong struggle with depression. Of those, 48 percent admitted to recurrent suicide ideation throughout their lives, and 16 percent said they had made at least one attempt.[2]

These numbers support the findings of numerous other studies. It's not hard to see why. People suffering from depression, for any number of reasons, already have one foot down the path to despair. I described the problem like this in my book *Healing Depression for Life*:

> Depression is real. And painful. And frightening.
>
> All too often, depression can even be life threatening, when it drains a person of hope to the point of considering self-harm. Beyond the toll it takes on individual lives, depression places enormous strain on families, businesses, schools, and governments. In fact, no corner of society is immune to its disabling effects.[3]

Psychosis. Research reveals a clear relationship between psychotic episodes—like those that occur in people suffering from schizophrenia—and the risk of suicide. A recent study published in the *Journal of the American Medical Association* reports that this is especially true among children. One of the study's authors, Evelyn J. Bromet, commented, "Worryingly, prospective studies of school-aged children have reported strong associations between [psychotic experiences] and suicide attempts, with children with [psychotic experiences] having an approximately 11-fold increased odds of suicide attempts during the following 12 months compared to those without [psychotic experiences]."[4]

What's more, a World Health Organization survey of nearly 34,000 adults in nineteen countries concluded that a psychotic experience nearly *doubles* a person's risk of suicide ideation and behavior.[5]

Substance Abuse Disorder. The link between intoxication or impairment and suicide can be described in a single word: *disinhibition*. That is, substances that adversely affect a person's judgment and risk aversion can make them more likely to form suicidal thoughts and then to *act* on them before sobering up. According to a 2016 report by the Substance Abuse and Mental Health Services Administration:

- Approximately 22 percent of deaths by suicide involved alcohol intoxication, with a blood-alcohol content at or above the legal limit.
- Opiates (including heroin and prescription painkillers) were present in 20 percent of suicide deaths, marijuana in 10.2 percent, cocaine in 4.6 percent, and amphetamines in 3.4 percent.

Furthermore, the report states, "Acute alcohol intoxication is present in about 30–40 percent of suicide *attempts*."[6]

Post-traumatic Stress Disorder. A well-known marker for elevated risk of suicide is exposure to traumatic mistreatment or events. These include victims of childhood abuse or neglect, sexual assault victims of any age, combat veterans, emergency first responders, and people who have witnessed mass violence or horrific accidents. Dr. Matthew Tull, a professor of psychology and a science writer, sheds light on why, reinforcing what we've already discussed: "Experiencing a traumatic event and/or developing PTSD can have a tremendous impact on a person's life. The symptoms of PTSD can make a person feel constantly afraid and isolated. In addition, depression is common following a traumatic event and among people with PTSD."[7]

Before we move on, be sure you understand this: the majority of people living with mental health challenges do not consider,

Jake Made Things Worse—Before He Made Them Better

"I started to think of my depression as being stranded on an alien planet where the force of gravity is ten times stronger," said Jake. "Everyone around you seems practically weightless by comparison, because they belong here and you don't."

Nine months after he pulled the trigger, Jake was still recovering from a self-inflicted gunshot wound that was meant to end his life. After many years battling chronic depression, he had finally given up—pushed past his limit by a toxic combination of poor mental health and a string of life crises.

At fifty, Jake faced his second divorce. His wife claimed she could no longer endure his "dark moodiness." In the process, he lost the ailing auto repair business he'd nursed along for more than a decade. Alienated from his kids and friends, Jake moved to a small town in Montana where he could "get away from it all."

"I guess I found out firsthand how true it is what they say—'wherever you go, there you are,'" Jake said, still trying to understand exactly how he reached a place where suicide seemed like his only choice.

After the freshness of his new home wore off, his depression flared up with a vengeance. Only now he was in an unfamiliar community with no support system of any kind. He started drinking more than usual. Then he was abruptly laid off from his new job as a bartender at a local hotel because of an economic downturn.

Lifelong depression that went mostly untreated. Divorce and isolation from his community. Sudden unemployment and financial uncertainty. Jake quickly slid down that slope from hopelessness to despair—and saw only one way to make the fear and pain go away.

"I've learned to see the ways I took a bad situation and made it much worse," Jake admitted. "I ran away from my problems instead of asking for help. I let booze do my thinking when things got tough. So, I'd say to people like me, 'Yeah, life can be really hard and unfair. That part you can't control. But some things you can. Put down the bottle. Pick up the phone. Don't be afraid to ask for help—tell people exactly what you need.'"

attempt, or complete suicide. These conditions do not make suicide a foregone conclusion. They are only a predictive marker that, together with other warning signs, can be a valuable tool in recognizing when someone needs extra help.

A Crisis of Fear or Loss

The scope of life events that might fit in this category is practically endless. In the CDC data above, "crisis in the past or upcoming two weeks" accounted for nearly a third of all suicides reported in the study. That could include:

- The death of a loved one, particularly a child
- Home foreclosure
- Bankruptcy
- Excessive debt
- Broken relationships
- Criminal investigation or conviction
- Job loss
- Marital strife or infidelity
- Bullying or cyberbullying
- Disappointment after failure to achieve a goal
- Natural disaster
- Political or social anxiety
- A damaging secret exposed

The list could go on and on—and could include anything that might cause a person to feel hopeless, trapped, isolated, or despairing. In fact, this group of potential triggers is so broad it ceases to be a "category" at all. The value in being aware of crisis as an impetus toward suicidal behavior is that it forces us to *pay attention* to what's going on in the lives of people around us—particularly those who may be vulnerable because of other factors in this list.

Poor Health

People with a terminal illness or a chronic and prolonged condition that leaves them disabled or in persistent pain have more reason than most to succumb to hopelessness and despair. A 2017 article in the online publication *ScienceDaily* sums up the issue in its very title: "Burden of Physical Health Conditions Linked to Increased Risk of Suicide." It states, "Researchers found that 17 physical health conditions, ailments such as back pain, diabetes, and heart disease, were associated with an increased risk of suicide. Two of the conditions—sleep disorders and HIV/AIDS—represented a greater than twofold increase, while traumatic brain injury made individuals nine times more likely to die by suicide."[8]

A less obvious effect of dealing with chronic illness leads directly to an associated suicide risk factor—feeling one is a burden to others. A person who is dependent on caregivers—often friends and family—may consider their suicide to be for the benefit of others.

A Cry for Help

While it's difficult to quantify this particular factor, it is interesting to note that "nine out of ten people who attempt suicide and survive do not go on to complete suicide at a later date."[9] This statistic encompasses people who reconsider their previous decision and those who weren't fully intent on the choice to end their life in the first place.

Throughout this chapter we've acknowledged that isolation is one of the key conditions contributing to a person's impulse to commit suicide. If ordinary means of communication have failed—or if a person has not felt able to express their distress to someone else—then a suicide attempt may be a nonverbal plea that is impossible to ignore. That doesn't mean the person is being consciously manipulative, though that certainly does happen on occasion. It suggests that they have reached the point where methods of last resort seem to be all they have left.

Reasons to Heal

The decision to end one's life is multifaceted and may have roots reaching all the way into early childhood. If you've lost someone to suicide, a clear reason may never emerge. Looking closely at some of these common possibilities, however, is useful for grounding our search for the means to heal this tragic national wound in *compassion*. Suicide isn't an inscrutable mystery. It grows out of real-world problems and circumstances that are familiar to us all.

The good news is, real problems have real solutions if we have the will and the faith to find them.

—4—

Who Is at High Risk?

Suicide Does Not Discriminate, but Some People Are More Vulnerable Than Others

It should be clear by now that the question this chapter asks has no simple answer. Think of it this way: if our quest to better understand suicide and its causes were a jigsaw puzzle, we would be forced to admit we're mixing pieces from different boxes.

Each chapter so far has outlined one significant puzzle piece—sources of big-picture societal distress; the most common life crises known to push people to their breaking point; and the latest science searching for tangible physical causes. At best, the picture we assemble will be incomplete—and that's understandable. Every new clue and fresh viewpoint brings us a little closer to the goal of helping people before they conclude suicide is the only option left.

This chapter adds one more piece—demographic statistics that examine suicide in terms of age, gender, ethnicity, occupation, and trauma history. When combined with what we've discussed already, this data will help clarify the image we're straining to see: Who in our personal sphere of attention is most in danger and in need of our help?

A word of caution is warranted at this point, however. The picture we're assembling strays perilously close to what law enforcement officials and civil rights advocates call "profiling." That is, using the most common characteristics of yesterday's known perpetrator to preemptively identify tomorrow's.

In the case of suicide prevention, what's wrong with that, we might wonder? We're talking about helping people, not detaining them for no other reason than they fit a profile. But in this context the danger is not who we might *include* in our web of concern but who we might *leave out* because they don't fit the statistical mold. Every single human being on earth is a unique creation. We are not data points or statistical patterns to be recognized.

As we'll see, it is true that some particular groups seem to struggle more than others. But that is not the definitive end of the story. Middle-aged white men (45 to 64 years of age) commit suicide more often than any other segment of society; but that doesn't mean we can dismiss the risk to a 43-year-old woman if she is showing other signs of need.

Here's the point: use all the risk factors and demographics I'm presenting as *guidelines* to hone your ability to recognize when someone needs help. Just don't let them blind you to the outliers—those people who don't fit the mold but are signaling distress all the same.

Remember to see people one at a time.

By the Numbers

With that in mind, here are the groups of people who stand out in suicide statistics as being at greater risk than most.

Middle-Aged White Men

This category exceeds all others by a wide margin—and is revealed in a combination of separate statistics:

- In general, white males account for 73 percent of all suicides each year.[1]
- Although females report attempting suicide 1.4 times more often than men, males are 3.6 times more likely to die by suicide than women.[2]
- In 2018, the highest suicide rate was measured among adults between the ages of 45 and 64, with roughly 20 suicide deaths per 100,000 population. (By contrast, that is nearly double the rate among people ages 15 to 24.) The peak rate is over 21 per 100,000 in the 52 to 59 age range.
- White people suffer the highest rate of suicide each year, exceeding 16 per 100,000 in 2018—compared to 6.61 among Blacks and 7.20 among Hispanics. American Indians and Alaskan Natives were closest with 13.42.[3]

All that adds up to a real problem among middle-aged white men. While more research is needed to find conclusive reasons why this is true, it is intuitively obvious that many of the pressures we've discussed so far may fall especially heavy on this group. Researchers acknowledge that some of those factors are common to both sexes—mental health issues, substance abuse disorders, and access to lethal means of self-harm—but some speculate that additional risks are more pronounced in men. "[These] factors are likely to be exacerbated by other risk-related characteristics that occur more frequently among males, such as the underreporting of mental health problems, a reluctance to seek help, engagement in interpersonal violence, distress from economic hardship (e.g., unemployment), and dissolution of intimate relationships."[4]

The truth is, in many countries males grow up learning to hide their troubles and minimize their pain. Being perceived as weak is often seen by men as worse than simply enduring whatever challenge they may be facing. In addition, men are likely to carry a disproportionate sense of responsibility for their perceived failures in life. We've seen that social isolation is a major contributing factor in suicide across all groups. But for men over fifty, "going it alone" may have been a way of life all along. When other pressures mount, it's the only way many know.

In an article titled "All-American Despair," journalist Stephen Rodrick touched on another reason for anguish among men— "white male bashing"—and also evoked the compassion that's necessary if we are to find our way to real understanding.

> It's easy to bash white middle-aged men in America. As a member of that privileged group, I'll admit that much of the bashing has been warranted: No group in the history of the world has been given and squandered more than the white man. Yet the American white man is responsible for enough suicides annually that Madison Square Garden could not hold all the victims. And no matter how privileged, that's somebody's dad, someone's friend, someone's brother and someone's husband.[5]

We might add: someone's neighbor, coworker, baseball coach, or Sunday school teacher. In other words, white men are *people*, with the same wounds and vulnerabilities as anyone. Vilifying them en masse is a form of prejudice that, on top of everything else, may be fueling the crisis in suicide that the numbers above reveal.

On a positive note, researchers are also giving thought to what can be done to interrupt an individual's trajectory toward suicide, including

> preventing exposure to violence in early developmental periods, such as bullying/peer victimization, childhood abuse, and domestic

violence; enhancing academic engagement and reducing school drop-out rates; mitigating or preventing persistent alcohol and drug misuse; and developing a diverse array of community-based programs that engage men who otherwise would not seek care in traditional health settings or in settings that provide care for mental or substance use disorders.[6]

In the meantime, raising family and community awareness of the problem of suicide among middle-aged white men is key to intervention and prevention.

Victims of Childhood Sexual Abuse

Childhood trauma can cause "epigenetic alteration" of how certain genes are expressed in adulthood—particularly those genes involved in stress management systems in the brain. Whatever the mechanism, research has revealed a link between childhood sexual abuse and suicidality later in life.

Sexual abuse and, to a lesser extent, physical abuse in childhood have both been consistently associated with suicidal behavior. Indeed, those reporting any traumatic experience in childhood show a two- to five-fold higher risk of being suicide attempters compared to those who do not.[7]

Stop for a moment and consider those numbers. A victim of abuse may be as much as *five times* more likely to commit suicide. Even if it only makes suicidality twice as likely, sexual abuse is a huge amplifier of risk. Estimates of the prevalence of sexual abuse among American girls under eighteen range from 19 to 25 percent. Among boys, the rate is thought to be around 8 percent, though some researchers believe cases involving males tend to be underreported.[8] Those figures represent a substantial number of people all across the world who struggle throughout their lives with the emotional and psychological consequences of abuse.

It should be obvious that secrecy and persistent shame can follow these people into adulthood. That complicates the efforts of others to recognize and respond to elevated suicide risk, because the truth so often remains hidden.

Military Veterans

At first glance, suicide rates among veterans appear to be declining—down from the much touted twenty-two-a-day figure a few years ago to the more recent seventeen a day, according to Veterans Administration statistics. However, an article in the *Military Times* points out the change is more about differences in how the numbers are gathered than any real decline. This is done by "removing active-duty, National Guardsmen and reservists from the larger number. State data had grouped all military together in the past. Again, VA officials are quick to point out that the new metric does not represent a decrease in veteran deaths, just a different way of presenting the information."[9]

Here are the numbers as of 2016, the most recent year for which data is available:

- The overall suicide rate for veterans is 1.5 times greater than nonveterans. Among female veterans it is 2.5 times higher.
- The suicide rate for veterans ages eighteen to thirty-four substantially increased from 2005 to 2016, from 24 to over 30 per 100,000.
- When comparing veteran suicide rates by age group, veterans ages eighteen to thirty-four had the highest suicide rate in 2016, at 45 per 100,000.
- In 2016, 58.1 percent of veteran suicides were among veterans age fifty-five and older.[10]

While the last item in the list certainly grabs attention—that nearly 60 percent of veterans who committed suicide were over

SURVIVORS SPEAK:
Francie's Search for the Right Questions about Veteran Suicide

"People talk about veteran suicide like it's some big mystery," said Francie, an office manager at a small tech firm in the Pacific Northwest. Her sister, Vivian, had died by suicide five years earlier, several months after leaving active duty military service.

"It's like, 'What's wrong with all these people who can't get back into civilian life?'" she continued. "'How can we help them adjust?' But for a lot of them, that's the wrong question."

Francie had made it her personal mission to study veteran suicide, to try and make sense of Vivian's death. The pair had been inseparable as children, always imagining they would marry two brothers and live in side-by-side houses. Even as young adults, they remained very close. That began to change soon after Vivian joined the army.

"Even before she was out of basic training her letters started to change," Francie recalled. "She got harder and more reserved. I tried to get her to talk about it during her first leave that Christmas, but she'd just tell me I didn't understand."

Vivian—a helicopter mechanic—spent the last thirteen months of a three-year enlistment in Korea.

"That's when she stopped really talking to me at all," Francie recalled.

Like many others involved in the effort to understand veteran suicide, Francie has concluded that the "right" question is not how to help veterans assimilate back into civilian life, but to wonder why military life can be so hard on some.

"When you read through a list of suicide risk factors, for some people you are looking at a description of being in the military," Francie said. "Isolation from people they love, constant traumatic stress, loss of fellow soldiers they care about, access to firearms and the know-how you need to use them, a culture of substance use to dull all that. It adds up."

Francie admits Vivian had never been in combat, so some of those things don't apply. What she did experience, however, practically from day one, was systematic sexual harassment and discrimination. In fact, reading through her sister's journals after her death gave Francie reason to suspect she'd been the victim of sexual assault while serving in Korea.

"Instead of wondering what our veterans need to get on with their lives, we should be asking them, 'Hey, what happened to you while you were in? Do you need to talk about that first?'"

fifty-five—it is the high rate among younger veterans that has officials most worried. The *Military Times* article continues:

"What we see is there is a specific problem with veterans and suicide," said Rajeev Ramchand, a research fellow with the Bob Woodruff Foundation who has worked closely on the issue. "There is a younger veteran problem, there is a female veteran problem. . . . I think the bigger question VA has to grapple with is why that younger number keeps getting worse."[11]

Yet the high suicide rate among veterans is not just a problem for the VA to grapple with. Those people, whatever their age or sex, live in communities all over America. It is up to caregivers and concerned people everywhere to understand the risk and be ready to respond with help.

Elderly People

In a previous chapter, we identified triggering conditions that contribute to suicidality, two of which are chronic health problems and feeling that one is a burden to others. It should come as no surprise, then, that adults over the age of sixty-five have a substantially higher suicide rate than the general population.

> Older adults are disproportionately likely to die by suicide. Comprising only 13 percent of the US population, individuals age 65 and older accounted for 18 percent of all suicide deaths in 2000. Among the highest rates (when categorized by gender and race) were white men age 85 and older: 59 deaths per 100,000 persons, more than five times the national US rate of 10.6 per 100,000.[12]

Again, notice that older white men are most at risk. Other contributing factors include social isolation, fixed income financial stress, recent loss of loved ones, and substance abuse disorder.

Teenagers

In 2018, the suicide rate among Americans between the ages of fifteen and twenty-four was 14.5 per 100,000. Unraveling the causes and contributing factors behind this horrifying statistic may present the biggest challenge of all. For that reason I address the topic separately in Appendix A at the end of the book.

By Occupation

Little solid research exists into why people with certain jobs are more at risk of suicide than others. Nevertheless, statistics reveal substantial correlation—and some results might surprise you. For example, health care workers in general—and psychiatrists in particular—are especially at risk. "Here in the US, physicians have the highest suicide rate of any profession (28 to 40 per 100,000), more than double that of the general population (12.3 per 100,000). What's more, of all the medical specialties, psychiatry is near the top in terms of suicide rates."[13] Similarly, dentists have been cited as another high-suicidal group as an occupation. Male dentists have a high suicide rate of 8.02, with female rates at 5.28.[14]

More study is needed to identify solid reasons for such high suicide rates among physicians. However, it's possible to speculate that doctors live and work in a stressful environment that takes a mental and emotional toll. Among the factors are job-related isolation and demands, responsibility for the health outcomes of others, difficulty maintaining a balance between work and home life, and financial pressures.

The Centers for Disease Control and Prevention compiled numbers for 2016 in a report called "Suicide Rates by Industry and Occupation."[15] Here are those professions with the highest risk (given in suicides per 100,000 among males only):

- Mining, quarrying, and oil and gas extraction—54.2
- Construction—45.3
- Other services (e.g., automotive repair)—39.1
- Agriculture, forestry, fishing, and hunting—36.1
- Transportation and warehousing—29.8

Among women, the arts, food service, and health care all showed elevated risk.

An Emphasis on Empathy

The purpose of these early chapters focusing on describing people who are "most at risk" of suicide is not to arm ourselves with a comprehensive checklist of warning signs and indicators. It is to put ourselves in the shoes of our family members, friends, and neighbors—to see the world through their eyes and feel the weight of their burdens and the pain of their wounds. If we'll train ourselves to do that with everyone we meet, we are more likely to notice distress when we see it. *Then*, knowing what we know about the tragedy of suicide, we'll be more likely to spot the warning signs that someone is in need of real help.

—5—

Setting the Record Straight

Unmasking Myths and Misconceptions about Suicide

"Sometimes I wonder if . . ." Roxy's voice trailed off.

"What?" asked her husband, Charlie. "You wonder what?"

"If she would ever, you know, hurt herself."

Roxy was referring to their daughter, Ronelle, who had seemed increasingly distant and depressed after a painful breakup.

Charlie couldn't believe his wife would think—much less say—such a thing. After he got over the shock, he shook his head. "Roxy, that's ridiculous. She's just a little depressed. She'll get over it in time. Besides, suicide is related to mental illness, and there's no mental illness in either of our families."

"I don't think it has to be related to mental illness," Roxy pushed back. "Besides, she's been making not-so-veiled references, talking about how the world would be better off without her. And one of her college friends committed suicide last year, remember? Maybe that's influencing her."

"Sweetheart, you're making a mountain out of a molehill. Suicide isn't contagious like the flu, you know? Besides, if she's talking about it, she's okay. People who are serious about something like that just do it—they don't talk about it. She's fine, Roxy. Trust me. She'll get over this. Look, can we talk about something else? How was your day?"

Charlie's reactions are hardly surprising. There is a stigma attached to suicide. It's uncomfortable to think about, and many people avoid talking about it. Unfortunately, this gives opportunity for myths and misconceptions to develop and persist.

The power of these myths and misconceptions is that they can drive actions and decisions that have devastating results. When we are misled, we can say and do things that don't help and can even exacerbate an already precarious situation. We can be lulled into not taking action when we should or spurred into taking the wrong action altogether.

Let's take a moment to debunk some of the most common myths about suicide.

Myth #1: "Suicide is a result of mental illness."

The truth is that many people who suffer with mental illness never consider suicide. And while it is true that suicidal thinking can be related to mental illnesses such as depression or addiction, often it isn't.

According to the National Alliance on Mental Illness, 46 percent of people who commit suicide have a known mental illness.[1] Conversely, 54 percent—more than half—do not. And while it's likely that undiagnosed disorders are playing a role in some of these cases, the fact remains that suicide can be driven by many factors, including medical conditions, recent loss or tragedy, and drug or alcohol abuse.

Resist the urge to look at what someone *doesn't* have and draw the conclusion that, as a result, they are immune from suicidal thoughts. And, as we'll discover as we look at other myths, neither can we look at what someone *does* have—success or fame, for example—and draw the same inaccurate conclusion.

This isn't to say that there are not signs, symptoms, and red-flag conditions—and mental illness is definitely a red-flag condition. But the mere absence of an obvious sign or a red-flag condition doesn't mean that someone you love isn't at risk.

Myth #2: "Talking about suicide or asking someone if they feel suicidal can plant the idea in their head and encourage them to do it."

Actually, the opposite is true. Asking someone about suicide does not encourage them to take that course of action. In fact, if someone has been having suicidal thoughts, the chance to talk about their thoughts and feelings with someone who cares may be a relief.

This is why suicide hotlines exist and why they are helpful.

Suicide is an attempt to find a permanent solution to what are often temporary problems. Someone who is considering suicide is in deep emotional pain and looking for relief. If a compassionate conversation can provide even a small level of relief, it can buy time for circumstances to change, hopeless feelings to subside, or help to arrive.

"Are you thinking of killing yourself?" is a direct way of starting a conversation. Less direct approaches include asking how someone is feeling or offering the observation that someone has seemed down or troubled lately. Due to the stigma surrounding suicide, people who are in enough pain to think about taking their own life may not know who to talk to or how to reach out, so an opening comment or question from you may be exactly what they need.

If you can get someone talking about their thoughts and feelings, let them talk. Be a good listener. Don't interrupt or lecture. Studies show that the simple act of sharing our thoughts and feelings can reduce stress, strengthen our immune system, and improve our mood. In fact, a brain imaging study out of UCLA shows that verbalizing feelings of sadness, anger, and pain makes those feelings less intense by calming a part of the brain called the amygdala.[2]

In other words, contrary to what the myth may suggest, broaching the subject of suicide may be the most important conversation you can have.

Myth #3: "If someone is talking about committing suicide, they're just looking for attention and are not in any real danger."

Actually, talking about suicide is one of the warning signs that someone *is* at risk, and their comments should be taken seriously.

If someone talks about feeling trapped or hopeless, shares that there's no reason to go on living, or suggests that the world would be better off without them, they are not seeking attention but signaling that they are in real distress.

People contemplating suicide are not longing to die, per se. What they want is for the pain and distress to go away. It's not that they don't want to live—they just don't want to live their current life any longer.

Seeking attention is rarely at the root of comments like these.

Myth #4: "People who die by suicide are selfish to take the easy way out."

It's not unusual for people, in the painful wake of the suicide of a loved one, to have this thought. And from their perspective it makes sense. After all, those left behind can face years—even a lifetime—of dealing with the aftermath. In this context, death may seem like the "easier" path, and the person who took that path can appear self-serving for doing so.

SURVIVORS SPEAK:
Jacquie Learns to Forgive Her Husband— and Herself

"When a friend suggested I try a grief support group, I wasn't even sure I'd be allowed into the group," Jacquie remembered, before explaining the reasons she felt she didn't belong.

"I assumed grief counseling was for people who'd lost someone recently, but my husband had committed suicide eleven years earlier. Plus, I felt there was a stigma attached to death by suicide—I was embarrassed to admit he hadn't loved me enough to stay and figure things out, that he had abandoned me by taking his own life."

Jacquie's husband had struggled with suicidal ideations for years before hanging himself one afternoon while Jacquie was on a business trip. She'd returned home from the airport and discovered his body in their garage.

More than a decade later, Jacquie was still reeling.

But the real reason she was afraid to seek out grief counseling groups was because, in her words, "I had a secret I didn't want anyone to know."

Jacquie was convinced that her husband's suicide was somehow her fault.

"We'd had a fight before I left," Jacquie adds. "If we hadn't argued, would he still be alive?"

The loss and guilt Jacquie felt over her husband's suicide festered until she began to wonder if the world would be better off without her too. She was ashamed to admit that she found herself increasingly thinking her own suicidal thoughts. Was that the answer? Would ending her own life put to rest her inability to move on after her husband's death?

Desperate, Jacquie finally made an appointment with a grief counselor. She also began attending a grief support group where she was surprised to discover there is no timeline for grief. She learned that struggling years after a loved one has died—especially if they have died by suicide—is not uncommon.

One-on-one counseling also helped her address the debilitating guilt. "My husband struggled with depression, bipolar disorder, and suicidal thoughts long before we met," Jacquie said. "He had been thinking about this a long time. His life didn't hinge on our argument that morning."

She also learned that people who lost a friend or relative to suicide are 65 percent more likely to attempt suicide than people who are bereaved due to natural causes. Knowing that her own thoughts of suicide were not unique went a long way toward alleviating the shame she'd felt—and fostering new hope.

Today Jacquie says that, for the first time in over a decade, she is able to feel hopeful about her future.

"I'll never know all the factors that led to his final decision, and I've accepted that at this point. What I do know is that he wouldn't have wanted me to live the rest of my life in the shadow of his final choice. And he definitely wouldn't have wanted me to spiral into my own suicidal thinking. More importantly, I don't want that for myself. It's taken more than a decade, but I'm learning how to give my husband—and myself—the grace we both deserve."

I believe people who survive the suicide of a loved one may buy into this myth for another reason: sometimes it's easier to blame than to grieve.

Anger is a strong emotion, and for a time it may displace the overwhelming emotions of pain, loss, and grief. If those who are left behind can convince themselves that a loved one made a selfish choice, the resulting anger may seem preferable to allowing themselves to experience and grieve the loss. Blame can be a protective buffer from the deep pain of grief.

Is suicide a selfish act? Actually, people who die by suicide often believe they have become a burden to people they care about and see their death as making life easier for those left behind. In this regard, they may see ending their own life as one of the most self-less choices they can make.

It's also important to remember that the level of extreme emotional distress that accompanies suicidal ideations distorts logical thinking. Someone who is considering suicide is processing information in ways that may not make sense to those who would be left behind.

Myth #5: "Someone who is successful and has their act together isn't at risk."

A simple look at headlines over the past decades refutes this myth. We are often stunned by the news of successful, high-profile people who have died by suicide in recent years. The list includes: Beloved comic and actor Robin Williams. Award-winning fashion designer Kate Spade. Celebrity chef Anthony Bourdain. Musician Avicii. YouTube star Stevie Ryan. NFL star Junior Seau. Film director Tony Scott. Sadly, this list could go on and on.

Why are successful people as susceptible to suicidal ideation as everyone else? For starters, factors like depression, personal loss, medical conditions, and drug or alcohol abuse are no respecter of persons—regardless of how successful or "together" someone seems.

In addition, personality traits and behaviors that sometimes empower success—like perfectionism or working long hours—can also contribute to stress, depression, and isolation. And studies show that creativity, another trait often associated with success, is linked with higher risk for mood disorders such as depression and bipolar disorder.

Finally, success itself creates stress and pressure. Maintaining an image of success or a high level of performance over time can be exhausting. Success can also invite scrutiny and judgment from others.

Living with the added stress, pressure, expectations, and scrutiny created by success can become overwhelming. And in the context of other risk factors, like mental illness or addiction, the lifestyle distresses can tilt the scale in a tragic direction.

Myth #6: "People decide to take their own life out of the blue and without warning."

Some suicides are indeed spontaneous decisions made in a moment when uncharacteristically hopeless feelings meet an unfortunate opportunity to take action.

Most of the time, however, there are warning signs. As we will discuss in chapter 6, these signs may be verbal or nonverbal, subtle or so sporadic it may be hard to take them seriously.

Talking about giving up or wanting to die, giving away personal belongings, withdrawing from relationships, expressing concern about being a burden to others, increased mood swings, and saying goodbye to people are all obvious warning signs.

But there are also conditions and events that can serve, if not as predictors, then as red flags. For example, if someone experienced childhood abuse, is living with a chronic illness, has a traumatic brain injury, has tried unsuccessfully to commit suicide in the past, or has experienced the loss of someone they love to suicide, this person may be more susceptible to suicidal ideations than you think.

A recent unexpected loss of a job, relationship, or financial stability can also set the stage for the kind of despair that can lead to suicidal thinking.

Finally, studies have shown a strong link between alcohol and drug abuse and attempted or completed suicides. In fact, people who abuse alcohol or drugs are at ten to fourteen times greater risk of dying by suicide.[3]

Are there always indications? No. But believing the myth that there are no signs can keep us from seeing the signs that are there.

Myth #7: "When someone starts to recover after hitting rock bottom, they are out of the woods."

I wish this were true. Unfortunately, there are many cases of suicidal people who have been admitted to a hospital or clinic, received help, and appeared to have made a turnaround, only to die by suicide upon their release.

Suicide takes a certain level of energy and presence that someone may not have at "rock bottom." As they begin to feel better, however, they may find themselves with the energy to take a self-destructive action before they have experienced healing in their thoughts and emotions.

In other words, someone who is starting to exhibit signs of improvement is still in need of observation and care from loved ones.

Recovery from suicidal thinking doesn't happen overnight. It takes time. The good news is that it can and does happen.

Myth #8: "Someone who is suicidal will always be suicidal."

People considering suicide are trying to solve a problem: the problem of overwhelmingly painful thoughts and emotions. As soon as they can experience relief from that problem, the suicidal thoughts will be reduced or eliminated as well.

What can provide relief? The possibilities are varied and include therapy, improved coping skills, a stronger support system, overcoming destructive habits, and addressing unresolved emotional hurts.

The point is that painful thoughts and emotions are treatable. And when they are treated, the internal pressure to escape the pain by suicide is relieved. Suicide is a last-ditch, desperate effort to make the pain stop. If the pain dissipates, suicidal ideations tend to dissipate as well.

Believing the myth "once suicidal, always suicidal" is dangerous because it destroys the hope of recovery. The truth is that people who have considered—even attempted—suicide can go on to live long lives characterized by health and healing.

If you love someone who is suicidal, there is cause for hope. And when you are informed and aware, you have greatly increased your chances of helping your loved one through this crisis and into a more hope-filled life on the other side.

PART 2

HELPING YOUR LOVED ONE MOVE BEYOND CRISIS and TOWARD WELLNESS

—6—

Signs and Symptoms

Red Flags That Should Put You on Red Alert

So far, I'll admit, I've been painting a picture of a person at elevated risk of suicide with very broad strokes. That was necessary to establish general boundaries and put us all on the same playing field. Risk indicators include such things as mental health status; a sudden financial or legal crisis; loss of a loved one or a key relationship; chronic health challenges; social isolation; history of trauma; genetic predilection; demographic profile; and professional affiliation.

But is it really practical to maintain a red-alert state of suicide watchfulness for every depressed person you're aware of? Or even for those people who exhibit concerning combinations of these general risk factors? No, not really. The vast majority of people struggling with such issues never go so far as suicide ideation, much less making concrete plans. So, armed with these general parameters of risk, is it possible to get more specific and spot those people who are giving suicide serious thought—or have even already made up their minds to end their life?

Fortunately, the answer is yes. This chapter reveals the more common warning signs that warrant increased vigilance on our part, and possibly even immediate intervention.[1] Like anything dealing with human thoughts and emotions, this list is not foolproof or exhaustive. But it does offer much-needed insight—drawn from the experiences of suicide survivors—into the suicidal state of mind and how to recognize it.

Interpreting Telegraphed Intention

Some of the following indicators can be hard to distinguish from the periodic reactions people have to our stressed and stretched modern way of life—like pouring an extra cocktail after a tough day, for instance, or being more likely to snap at the kids. But as you'll hear in testimonials, there is an alarming quality to these behaviors in someone who is considering suicide that seems obvious—*after* the fact. In this respect, raising your awareness is an exercise in honing your skills of observation and learning to notice signals that are hiding in plain sight. The goal is to develop *insight* and avoid the pain of regretful *hindsight*.

That said, there are a few such warnings that are glaringly apparent and need no interpretive intuition. Let's start there.

Clear and Present Signs

A recent suicide attempt. While a small percentage of suicide attempts may qualify as a cry for help and not reflect a real desire to die, statistics reveal that trying once makes it far more likely the person will try again.[2] In any case, it is very difficult to tell the difference by observation alone—meaning all previous suicide attempts must be taken as evidence of elevated future risk.

Suicide talk or social media posts. Again, it is tempting to dismiss this kind of signal as an overly dramatic call for attention.

But when the topic of suicide or death makes it into a person's public discourse—even if only in casual references—it is time to pay special attention. Suicide talk includes:

- Suicide threats: "Maybe I'll kill myself and see how you like that." "You'll be sorry when I'm gone."
- Expressing a preoccupation with death: "I wonder what it feels like to die?" "Do you believe in hell?"
- Apologizing for being a burden: "Everyone will be better off without me around."

Often, the subject is couched in dark humor or obvious hyperbole, but that doesn't make it any less serious.

Taking steps to research or acquire lethal means. It is legal to own a gun in America, and lots of people do own one for legitimate reasons. But any sudden interest in firearms—especially from someone who already is part of an at-risk population—is a clear warning sign that suicide ideation may have moved into planning. This is true of unexplained interest in other lethal means as well—prescription drug dosages, types of poison and their effects (including illegal drugs), the mechanics of asphyxiation, access to tall buildings, and so on.

These kinds of clues are often subtle—gleaned from bits of overheard conversation or glimpsed internet searches—but the danger they represent is real and warrants immediate attention.

Saying goodbye. Often, people who have decided to end their lives will feel compelled to seek closure with people they care about—without giving away their plans. A sudden and uncharacteristic uptick in heartfelt communication from someone in your life—similar to what you might expect on the eve of a long absence—can be exactly what it seems: a final goodbye. Resist the temptation to chalk this up to sudden sentimentality, especially if you have any other reason to believe your loved one is under strain.

Simply asking the question, "Are you trying to say goodbye?" can often initiate a more honest conversation—or at least kick your observational intuition into gear.

Reading between the Lines

In contrast to the above, here are some signals that are more tenuous and take an extra measure of awareness to spot. I've included a few vignettes drawn from survivors' personal experiences to illustrate how some of these signs might look in real life.

Sudden improvement in mood. It seems counterintuitive that a decision to kill oneself can actually *improve* a person's outlook on life, yet that is precisely what many people exhibit once their choice is made.

Sheila had what her family dubbed an "Eeyore personality"—named for the gloomy and eternally pessimistic character in A. A. Milne's Winnie the Pooh stories. In truth, Sheila had suffered from major depression and anxiety for years, but without getting the help she needed. Her parents and siblings had long ago resigned themselves to her dark moods, and no one truly enjoyed her presence at family gatherings because she was a downer. So when she arrived for family dinner one week with a bright smile and positive outlook for once, no one bothered to wonder why—they simply gratefully received it as a sign that Sheila might finally be turning a corner.

"If only we'd seen that for what it was," Sheila's mother said after her daughter died by sleeping pill overdose. "It's hard to say to someone you love, 'Hey, why are you so happy all of a sudden?' But how I wish I had done that now."

Getting affairs in order. As we've already seen, closure is often important to someone who has decided to end their life. This manifests as a need to say goodbye, but also to tie up loose ends in their lives. They create a will and make sure someone knows where to find it. They tidy up financial records, return borrowed items, repay lingering debts, or cancel magazine subscriptions. On the surface all

Recognizing an Imminent Suicide Is Often a Team Effort

"Our story is a great example of the saying that 'it takes a village,'" Glenda told me. "Only in this case it's not to raise a child, it's to save a life. I don't think just one of us alone would have seen what was going on."

Glenda is a dispatcher at a Texas trucking company with about fifty employees. Heading into the holiday season in 2018, the warehouse foreman started acting strangely.

"Colton has always been a little different. Keeps to himself and is kind of moody," Glenda said. "But he shows up on time and does his work. In this business that makes him a star. So when he started coming in late pretty often, I noticed."

Glenda said she knows "the holidays can be hard on folks," so she decided not to pry. Then Frank, one of the delivery drivers, casually shared a story in the break room that made her think again. The night before he'd seen Colton pick a fight in a nearby bar with two oil field workers, for no apparent reason.

"'Like he wanted a beating,' is how Frank put it," said Glenda. "I've never heard Colton so much as raise his voice, so now I was really curious."

The tipping point came when Colton's daughter called to speak with him and mentioned to Glenda that he had not been returning her calls recently.

"That's when the light went on that something must be really wrong," Glenda said. "I said that to Colton's girl and told her about his fight. We agreed then and there to have a chat with him."

Confronted with a direct question about how he was doing, Colton broke down and admitted he had lost all hope in his life and had been thinking of "ending the misery." He agreed to submit himself for evaluation at the community hospital emergency room, where his long road to recovery began.

"I think that happened because we all three noticed something out of the ordinary and thought enough to say it out loud to somebody," Glenda said. "If we had just ignored it or figured it was none of our business, Colton might not be alive right now."

this looks admirably responsible and organized, but in combination with other suicide risk factors and warnings, it can signal exactly the opposite: a decision to escape everything once and for all.

"When Alex started giving away his tools, we all thought he was upgrading and getting rid of old stuff," said Marcus, a supervisor at a major East Coast construction company. "I offered to pay him for things he gave me, but he refused."

Then he tried to give one of his coworkers the keys and title to his truck, and Marcus saw a red flag. He had recently sat through mandatory company training for supervisors about the alarming rate of suicide in the construction industry.

"We got him into counseling, then he left the company," said Marcus. "I lost track of him, but I still worry about him from time to time."

Increased self-destructive behavior. The desire to commit suicide may first show up as a game of Russian roulette with the world—daring extreme circumstances (of their own making) to do the job. That can take many forms, including the unsafe practice of adventure sports, reckless driving, risky sex, criminal activity, a dramatic increase in substance use and abuse, and starting fights. In our culture, the entertainment media have created a cult of awe and admiration for this sort of adventurous character—someone who throws caution to the wind and lives life on their own terms. That makes it easy to miss what this person may be really saying—that they don't want to live at all.

"My brother was a serious climber, smart and dedicated to the sport," said Olivia. Stan was also an entrepreneur who started a climbing products company with several ideas in development.

"When the economy tanked and the business went bankrupt, his whole outlook changed," said Olivia. "It ate him up that he lost the savings our mom had invested."

Suddenly Stan started undertaking dangerous climbs without backup, then free climbing with no ropes or supports. And he returned to taking hard drugs that he had long ago left behind.

"I tried talking to him, but he shut me out," Olivia said. "The coroner listed his death as 'accidental overdose,' but I will always believe he killed himself."

Extreme emotional swings. I've described some people for whom the decision to commit suicide actually calms them down or prompts them to dispassionately set their affairs in order. For others, it unleashes a maelstrom of emotion that they have trouble managing. These people swing wildly from anger and rage to grief to crippling anxiety to unbridled happiness—all in short periods of time. Often, especially in a work environment, this behavior is seen as a disciplinary issue rather than a mental health crisis.

For example, in the weeks after Cameron's divorce was finalized, personnel records indicated he had become a "disruptive influence" on the factory floor where he worked. He developed a "manic" personality, his supervisor wrote, "one minute laughing and telling jokes, the next crying at his station."

When Cameron threw a heavy wrench at a coworker, he was placed on probation and forced to accept a strict ninety-day improvement plan to address "deficiencies." A week later he died from a self-inflicted gunshot wound. It's reasonable to wonder how the story might have been different had someone in Cameron's circle recognized the true source of his emotional swings.

Increased isolation. The truth is, Americans are increasingly disconnected from one another in general—a trend driven by social media and of necessity made much worse by the COVID-19 pandemic. Consider this from a 2020 study published in the *Journal of the American Medical Association Psychiatry*:

> Suicidal thoughts and behaviors are associated with social isolation and loneliness. Therefore, from a suicide prevention perspective, it is concerning that the most critical public health strategy for the COVID-19 crisis is social distancing. Furthermore, family and friends remain isolated from individuals who are hospitalized, even when their deaths are imminent. To the extent that these

strategies increase social isolation and loneliness, they may increase suicide risk.[3]

Decreasing social connection in general and government-mandated social distancing both make it much harder to spot when someone abruptly chooses to cut themselves off from meaningful contact with others. In the bustle of daily life, it's hard to keep track of the last time you heard from a loved one or friend or to notice when they stop posting on social media. Yet a person considering or planning suicide often goes into hiding as a way to reinforce their resolve or prevent anyone from noticing their distress and intervening—the very opposite of those who talk or post openly about their suicidal thoughts.

Cultivate the awareness to notice when someone who is otherwise at high risk suddenly drops off the radar.

Disrupted sleep patterns. Researchers have long recognized an association between depression and sleeping problems, so some have suggested that a reported link between suicide risk and insomnia (an inability to sleep) or hypersomnia (excessive sleepiness) only points to the underlying mental disorder and is therefore not a reliable predictor of suicidality. Some disagree, however. A 2015 article in *Psychiatric Times* asks:

> What explains these associations, especially when two seemingly opposite phenomena such as insomnia and hypersomnia are linked to suicide? One explanation is the simple concept of "burden of illness." It is well known that a chronic medical illness is a risk factor for suicide, so perhaps the burden of living with insomnia or hypersomnia becomes the "straw that breaks the camel's back."[4]

The author goes on to urge caregivers to take seriously a patient who reports "new or escalating" sleeping problems, and to query them "regarding the presence of suicide ideation."[5] That's good advice for anyone seeking to cultivate awareness of suicide risk in someone they care about. Severely disrupted sleep—one way or another—is a major red flag and compelling reason to actively intervene.

Expressing hopelessness. Earlier in chapter 3 I wrote, "A person who is at risk of self-harm as a result of some crisis has concluded that there is no way their circumstances will ever improve—that everything good about the life they had known is gone forever, beyond salvaging. Worse, whatever pushed them to that misguided belief has poisoned their future as well. No past to return to + no future to look forward to = *no hope.*" I made the point that all suicidal behavior originates in the belief that there is no way out and no way things will ever improve. This is the bedrock of suicide.

So when someone openly expresses their feelings of hopelessness, it is not the time for platitudes or motivational tactics. It's a call to listen—really listen—and respond as if someone's life depends on it.

"The last thing I said to my father was, 'Cheer up, Dad! Tomorrow's a new day,'" Roger told me through his tears, his voice catching on every word. "I suppose it's what he would have said to me when I was a teenager involved in some stupid drama."

Like many middle-aged men, Roger's dad, Felix, had an aversion to sharing his feelings with anyone. But that day he'd admitted to his son that he was "bone tired" and "out of reasons to hope for a better life."

Felix fatally shot himself a day later. "I'd give absolutely anything to have that moment back," Roger said.

Expressions of hopelessness can take many forms:

"I'll never get over what happened."

"I just feel like giving up."

"There's no point in trying so hard anymore."

"It's too late for me."

"What do I have to look forward to?"

81

These are not simple statements of Eeyore gloom, as Sheila's family might have said. They are painful admissions of real distress. They are visible evidence that a powerful precursor to suicide—hopelessness—is already taking shape in someone's mind. We ignore it at their peril—and ours.

Toward a Different Outcome

The good news—yes, there is good news—is that tragedy need not be the inevitable destination when someone reaches this level of despair. Awareness of all these risk factors and warning signs adds up to a real opportunity to save lives—and to *improve* life for everyone and make hopelessness a much rarer condition. That is the promise of the faith we are called to—when coupled with our own determination to embody God's love on earth.

When Jesus was tested by an expert in the law with the question, "What is the greatest commandment?" he replied, "'Love the Lord your God with all your heart and with all your soul and with all your mind.' This is the first and greatest commandment. And the second is like it: 'Love your neighbor as yourself'" (Matt. 22:37–39).

Healing our national suicide crisis starts—and ends—with loving our neighbor as ourselves.

—7—

Descent into Darkness

Understanding the Downward Spiral toward Suicide

In the last chapter we examined signs and symptoms that could signal a loved one's inclination toward a suicide attempt. I'll emphasize again that these red flags should be taken seriously. Usually, they become apparent toward the end of a long, agonizing inner battle—which means that an actual attempt may be near and the time for intervention may be waning.

Sadly, family and friends often miss that private inner struggle—or if they notice, they may dismiss it as a bad day or an unfortunate event that won't seem as bad in the morning. It's important for you to know that few troubled people simply wake up one day and decide to attempt suicide. With the exception of severe mental illness, such as schizophrenia, an attempted suicide usually follows a mental and emotional spiral that gradually pulls the victim further and further downward into darkness. As each stage brings deeper and deeper pain, the individual's desperate desire to end the suffering becomes more tempting, eventually appearing as the only option to find relief.

The Downward Spiral

In the pages ahead, I will show you how that downward spiral typically plays out. By knowing its stages and how people look and act in each one, you may be able to help your loved one deal with the problem in its less-severe stages and prevent it from deteriorating into the more critical, life-and-death stages. And while you may be able to help alleviate your loved one's suffering at the early stages, please do not hesitate to seek the help of a suicide helpline or a qualified counselor—better safe than sorry, even in what may appear to be the milder stages of the crisis.

Stage 1: Disappointment

This stage of the downward spiral may appear harmless, and it often is. The individual may experience disappointment over something that hasn't gone their way, whether big or small. Perhaps someone canceled a get-together they were looking forward to, or they didn't qualify for a loan, or a potential date declined, or they didn't receive due recognition for a job they'd just completed. These are all common occurrences in life and are, typically, easily recoverable.

But for someone who already struggles with self-doubt and self-worth issues, life's relatively benign disappointments can dig more deeply into the psyche. Instead of passing them off as a normal part of life, the sufferer takes note, overthinks, internalizes, and assigns hurt to the negative event. They feel let down. Perhaps even disillusioned: *I thought he was my friend. I'll never get ahead. She doesn't like me. They don't recognize how hard I work for them.*

Disappointment = Feeling let down and taking it personally.

84

Your loved one may or may not express these thoughts verbally. If they do, or if you sense that a disappointment is bothering them, you may be able to help them process it in a healthy way. Do not try to minimize the hurt with a flippant dismissal ("These things happen," or "You'll get over it," or "Just let it go"), because the situation doesn't seem flippant to them. It's digging into their mind and may become lodged there. Instead, empathize by saying something such as, "I'm sorry. You must feel disappointed." Casually help them acknowledge and verbalize what they're feeling.

"In spite of whatever disappointing experiences come our way, our challenge will be to not let bitterness take root," writes psychologist Manfred F. R. Kets de Vries in the *Harvard Business Review*. "When we become preoccupied by bad news, we lose sight of what is right in our lives and in the world around us."[1]

The comment by Dr. de Vries touches on an important principle: You can help your loved one refocus on what is right in their life and in the world. "I can understand your disappointment, but what's good about this?" "You still have the job, right? They obviously like your work even if they sometimes fail to commend you." Help the person you're concerned about look beyond the initial hurt to find and focus on the innumerable blessings in their life. They are there.

You can also assist a disappointed friend by helping them keep the disappointment in perspective. "You know, when I feel let down like that—and believe me, it happens—I've found that the key is to never take it personally. If others drop the ball or don't come through as you'd hoped, it's on them, not you. Maybe it was just not a good time for them. What's a healthy choice you can make to put this aside?"

Then offer to take your friend to lunch or coffee, a movie, or another favorite activity to help shift their attention away from the initial hurt. Your goal at the disappointment stage is to do what you can to help prevent it from becoming septic and degenerating to the next stage.

Stage 2: Discouragement

"We would do well to keep in mind that although disappointment is inevitable," de Vries warns, "being discouraged is always a choice."[2]

For someone prone to melancholy and overthinking, unresolved disappointment can become more deeply entrenched in the form of discouragement. Discouragement whispers that nothing has been going right and isn't likely to change anytime soon. Victims may feel dispirited and demoralized—disincentivized to try again at whatever has disappointed them: *"Obviously, she doesn't want to hang with me. I'm done hoping for dates." "I'll never get ahead financially. I won't work so hard next time."*

Writer William Ward defines discouragement this way:

Discouragement is dissatisfaction with the past, distaste for the present, and distrust of the future. It is ingratitude for the blessings of yesterday, indifference to the opportunities of today, and insecurity regarding strength for tomorrow. It is unawareness of the presence of beauty, unconcern for the needs of our fellowman, and unbelief in the promises of old. It is impatience with time, immaturity of thought, and impoliteness to God.[3]

While that definition may seem a bit harsh, I believe the writer has accurately described the potential destruction that can occur when a person's disappointment is allowed to metastasize into full-blown discouragement. If unresolved, discouragement can turn the victim's entire perspective on life inside out and upside down.

> Discouragement = Feeling demoralized,
> disincentivized . . . and alone.

But keep in mind that discouragement is a choice. It doesn't attack from out of the blue. When you experience disappointment, you choose whether to obsess it into discouragement. To

7 Powerful Promises to Battle the Downward Spiral

Scripture is clear that our Creator wants his children to live in a state of joy and hope. God cares so much for our mental and emotional health that he has provided multiple assurances for those who struggle with any of the issues we're addressing in this chapter.

Below are seven God-given promises straight from Scripture. You can help a struggling friend by going through these and other hope-filled Scriptures with them, reflecting together how a particular promise applies to their situation, and how God's promised help can strengthen them to be an overcomer.

1. "I praise you because I am fearfully and wonderfully made; your works are wonderful, I know that full well" (Ps. 139:14).
2. "And we know that in all things God works for the good of those who love him" (Rom. 8:28).
3. "'For I know the plans I have for you,' declares the Lord, 'plans to prosper you and not to harm you, plans to give you hope and a future'" (Jer. 29:11).
4. "Those who hope in the Lord will renew their strength. They will soar on wings like eagles; they will run and not grow weary, they will walk and not be faint" (Isa. 40:31).
5. "Do not fear, for I am with you; do not be dismayed, for I am your God. I will strengthen you and help you; I will uphold you with my righteous right hand" (Isa. 41:10).
6. "Rejoice always; pray without ceasing; in everything give thanks; for this is God's will for you in Christ Jesus" (1 Thess. 5:16–18 NASB).
7. "Cast all your anxiety upon him because he cares for you" (1 Pet. 5:7).

Now take these promises a step further by offering to memorize one together: "If you could choose just *one* of these verses as your empowering promise for when you feel down, which would it be?" When you and your friend memorize a Scripture together and review it often, out loud, you'll form a special bond over "our verse." More importantly, they will have an assuring, empowering verse at the ready to elevate their spirits and assure them that they are not alone.

Claiming God's promises and quoting them aloud is a powerful refutation of the fatalistic garbage that's clawing for a foothold in the mind. It reminds us of our Creator's incredible desire to help us overcome troubled thoughts. He's there, and he cares. We should readily accept his invitation to "cast all your anxiety upon him because he cares for you."

forgive and let go is the healthy choice; to linger on the initial hurt is to willingly take a step downward to wallow in the self-pity of discouragement.

Encourage your friend to choose to forgive and release whatever brought on the disappointment or discouragement. This will help them reorient their thinking from victim to overcomer, from self-pity to strength. (See the "7 Powerful Promises" sidebar on the previous page.)

Discouragement is a harmful choice. If your friend chooses to continue letting discouragement and self-pity dominate their thinking, they open their heart to stage 3 of the deadly spiral.

Stage 3: Diminishment

This stage centers on feeling disrespected or put down. Other appropriate descriptions include *disparaged*, *denigrated*, *demeaned*, and *devalued*. Each makes the individual feel lessened as a person. If you feel devalued, you feel you're of less value to someone than you once may have been. This could be a friend, coworker, boss, spouse, or dating partner—even God. Sadly, school bullying or cyberbullying among teens is a tragic extreme example of intentional diminishment that has become all too real in our society and has resulted in innumerable teen suicides or attempted suicides.

For other strugglers, there may or may not have been hostile intent, but something was said or implied that ripped into the victim's already-raw sensibilities. If prior disappointment and discouragement have not been dealt with, their spirit may be especially tender when a perceived put-down comes their way.

> Diminishment = Feeling put down, devalued, disrespected; that you don't matter.

And it hurts. Badly. It cuts deeper into an existing open wound. Your friend feels marginalized by someone whose opinion matters to them.

You can help by assuring them that you believe in them . . . and so does their Creator. Psalm 139:14 assures us that we are "fearfully and wonderfully made" by God, which means we are valued and precious in God's sight. You can encourage your friend, "When you feel put down or diminished by someone, tell yourself 'I am fearfully and wonderfully made. I matter.' That comes straight from God."

The next step is a tough one, but it may be the most effective way to heal the hurt of diminishment. It is sometimes helpful and healing for your friend to try to talk with the person who offended them. If they decide to do this, they must do so in a calm, gentle way, even with a humble smile. It's critical to use "I" statements instead of accusatory "you" statements. For example:

"I want to be sure you and I are all right. . . . We got into a debate in this morning's meeting and things got a little heated. When I expressed my view and you replied, 'Whatever,' I felt some hurt—it felt like my input wasn't valued."

This takes courage . . . and humility. Hopefully the offender will respond with assurances that, of course, they value your friend's perspective and want them to speak up in meetings. Perhaps they can talk further about how to better handle heated disagreements in the future. Your friend could ask forgiveness for assuming that the other person meant harm, which may lead to the other person asking your friend's forgiveness as well.

Offer to role-play the conversation beforehand. With your coaching and moral support, your friend may be able to halt the downward spiral by turning hurt-filled diminishment into a healthier relationship. (Please understand that, depending on the situation, approaching someone who has committed an offense may not be advisable. This is often true in cases of physical or psychological abuse. When this is the case, seeking guidance from a qualified counselor is essential. See my book *Healing the Scars of Emotional Abuse* for specific information on this topic.)

The Later Stages: Harbingers

The last three stages of the downward spiral are the most precarious of the six—and usually are more noticeable to concerned friends. Any of these can be harbingers of an attempted suicide. If you suspect that your friend has descended into any of the following stages, they are in need of professional help. Find professional counseling and see that your friend gets there. They will also need your continued encouragement and support in these crucial stages.

Stage 4: Depression

To the troubled soul, unresolved discouragement and diminishment eats away at self-worth like a school of piranhas. As the struggler's mental, emotional, and physical strength continues to fray, they become less able to generate and sustain a positive outlook on life—or on themselves. They feel as if a weighted cloud hovers over them and presses them down. They feel worthless.

SURVIVORS SPEAK:
An Angel's Anguish

Kids can be sweet and wonderful. But a few can be cruel. And when they gang up in cruelty, it can be savage.

Fourteen-year-old Angela was one of the sweet ones. In fact, her mother, Allison, had nicknamed her "Angel." The name stuck, even among Angel's acquaintances and teachers.

Angel seemed to have a perpetual smile. She dressed nicely, treated others with respect and courtesy, and studied hard in school. She usually sat in the front third of the class, asked good questions, and offered thoughtful answers. Teachers commented more than once that Angel's parents were doing something right.

The bullying started on a midwinter school day when a student in one of Angel's classes posted a rude remark about her on social media. Something about Angel's mom doing her homework for her and dressing her each morning. Relatively benign, but still hurtful and completely unwarranted, especially for a girl so considerate and conscientious.

The next day this student posted again: "Did you see what little angel girl wore to school today? That ugly outfit seemed appropriate for the person who wore it!" The first post had been bad enough, but this one dug deeper. Angel wondered what was going on . . . what she may have done to incur the derogatory comments.

Unfortunately, like a spark from a tiny bit of kindling, the bullying burst into fire. Friends of the first student joined in, "liking" her slurs and adding their own disparaging comments. There were more remarks about Angel's looks, her sexuality, even her monthly cycle. In the hallways between classes, Angel was assailed by nasty put-downs. Once, as three girls walked by together, one reached out and deliberately knocked Angel's backpack from her shoulder.

Much as she wanted to be strong, Angel couldn't hold back the hurt—or the tears. What was happening? Why?

This is when she let her mom know. "At first I tried to minimize it for her," Allison admits. "Sometimes kids are mean, but then they move on. I told Angel not to let it bother her, to stay strong. That was a huge failure on my part."

One day after classes, the gang of three shoved Angel against the wall—hard. The biggest one pointed a finger in her face and threatened, "We're just getting started. And we're here all year." Then came texts and late-night phone calls: "Next time I see you I'm gonna flatten your nose." "We're gonna beat you up."

Angel's smile no longer graced her face. Unable to concentrate on her studies, her grades declined. As did her appetite. As did her sleep. Despondency and fear had taken over. Allison, realizing her daughter was in trouble, alerted the school principal to the bullying. The principal called in the three girls for a stern talk . . . which only inflamed their rage into retribution.

"We found her in the tub late one evening," Allison says, tears streaming. "The water was red. Our Angel had reached her limit. She had taken a knife from the kitchen and sliced her wrists to the bone."

Allison and her family say the heartache will never end. "I wish I had gone beyond just trying to reassure her that everything would eventually be okay—and beyond talking to the principal. I wish I had realized how much agony Angel was in. I wish I had gotten her immediately into counseling. I wish I had moved her to another school. *Please*, anyone out there, read the signs. Get help *now*."

Lethargic. Hopeless. While they need people—affirming, reassuring people—the last thing they want is to be around people. They are so, well, *alone*. A desire to escape nibbles at the edges of their consciousness.

They have descended into depression, and they feel that no one will understand.

It's true that those who have never experienced depression have a hard time understanding the condition. They may regard it merely as a bad mood or tough stretch—something you can snap out of. But depression is far heavier than that. A friend of mine who struggles with recurring depression describes it this way:

"You just want to withdraw and stay in bed, pull the covers over your head, and sleep—hoping you'll feel better when you wake up. Sometimes you feel better, but most often you don't."

Another description, offered by Elizabeth Wurtzel in *Prozac Nation*, says, "That's the thing about depression. . . . A human being can survive almost anything, as long as she sees the end in sight. But depression is so insidious, and it compounds daily, that it's impossible to ever see the end."[4]

> Depression = An oppressive sadness;
> a prolonged state of hopelessness, worthlessness,
> loss of interest, and aloneness.

Depression is real. And it can be very serious. For most cases, medical help and/or professional counseling is strongly recommended. But how can a friend like you be of help?

"Let your loved one know that you want to understand how he or she feels," advises the Mayo Clinic. "When the person wants to talk, listen carefully, but avoid giving advice or opinions or making judgments. Just listening and being understanding can be a powerful healing tool."[5] You can also remind your friend of their positive qualities and how much they mean to you and others.

People experiencing depression are often embarrassed by the "depression" label. They hope that willpower or the passage of time will make things better. "But depression seldom gets better without treatment and may get worse," advises the Mayo staff.[6] Encourage your loved one to seek help from a physician or mental health provider. You may need to set the appointment and accompany them. Qualified health providers can formalize the diagnosis and recommend ways to manage and mitigate the depression; a medical doctor or psychiatrist can also prescribe appropriate antidepression medications. (For a thorough discussion of this topic, see my book *Healing Depression for Life*.)

Stage 5: Despair

When diminishment and depression remain unresolved, the troubled mind can take on even more acute anguish and pain—to the point of despair. Despair is a derivative of the words *desperate* and *desperation*, which gives us a disquieting clue as to the severity of the condition. If your friend is experiencing despair, they are desperate. They are tormented by powerful feelings of inadequacy and failure. They feel hopeless and incapable of recapturing whatever semblance of normalcy they once enjoyed. They don't know where to turn, and they may have lost all motivation to try.

The desire to escape grows more insidious. They may be vulnerable to the lure of illicit drugs—anything to provide respite from the inner turbulence. Some of the portentous red-flag signs we listed in chapter 6, such as talking about "ending it all," giving away possessions, or saying goodbye to friends and family, may become evident now.

> Despair = Severe distress. Feelings of inadequacy, hopelessness, and failure. Overwhelming desire to escape. Condition critical. Red lights are flashing!

Continue to affirm and encourage your loved one. To help them verbalize hope, try to get them to review those Scripture promises aloud with you. Ask again what the verses mean to them and how they help them. *But you must not stop there.* Check around for the best mental-health professional you can find and share your concern. Set an appointment for your friend as soon as possible. Make sure they get there. Book a series of appointments and ask the counselor how you can be of help between appointments.

Please take despair very seriously. It can be the harbinger of suicide or attempted suicide. Your friend needs professional intervention *now*.

Stage 6: Destruction

> Destruction = Strongly thinking about
> or preparing to attempt suicide. Condition critical.
> Lights flashing and alarm bells sounding!

You've seen the sad statistics; we don't want your loved one to reach the destruction stage. But the disquieting reality is that some strugglers become suicidal despite the best preventive efforts. Should your friend be among them, please consider them in imminent danger, seek immediate professional help, and stay with them until help arrives.

Watch and Be Ready

This chapter describes the descent into darkness—the downward spiral that can lead to despair and suicide. Recognizing the stages will enable you to watch for further signs that foreshadow potential suicide—and be ready to step in. In chapter 8, I'm going to show you practical ways to intervene with a suicidal friend. Study and underscore them so you'll be prepared if that frightful moment should come.

But first, I want to speak directly to you about . . . *you*.

—8—

Step In and Speak Up

What to Do When You Believe
Someone Is Suicidal

Every word in this book so far has formed a trail of bread crumbs leading to this trove of knowledge: what you can *do* when you suspect someone close to you may be in danger of self-harm.

Without this step, all you've learned—about the worsening reasons for societal distress, rising suicide rates, at-risk populations, and common warning signs—will have been merely an academic exercise. It's time to close the loop and answer the pivotal question that's been implied all along: How do we intervene effectively when someone has reached such a depth of hopelessness and despair that ending their life seems like the only way out?

Fortunately for us, the answer does not lie in uncharted territory. A lot of excellent research and clinical experience has gone into creating an intuitive and reliable intervention map. It's a series of checkpoints that will serve to keep us focused on what matters most—helping someone in great pain find their way back from the precipice.

In a moment I'll share six steps that I've adapted from the National Suicide Prevention Lifeline's #BeThe1To program.[1] First, however, there are a few important things to keep in mind as we go.

Rules of the Road

1. If observation and intuition tell you someone is at risk, don't second-guess yourself.

It's a rare thing for any of us to face life-and-death decisions—so it's all too easy to dismiss legitimate concerns as overly dramatic or blown out of proportion. But this is not the time for hesitation or adopting a wait-and-see attitude. If you sense trouble but feel reluctant to speak up because of self-doubt, ask yourself: What have I got to lose? Compare that to what you and your loved one have to *gain* from a timely intervention.

2. Talking about suicide does not "plant" the idea in someone's mind.

I mentioned this point in chapter 5, and it's worth repeating: many people are reluctant to raise the subject of suicide when someone is in distress for fear that they may be giving the person ideas they wouldn't have considered on their own. That has even been the case among professionals, like school counselors, who have often hesitated to overtly screen students for suicide ideation. However, research has clearly dispelled this notion. One such study concluded, "Our findings suggest acknowledging and talking about suicide may in fact reduce, rather than increase suicidal ideation, and may lead to improvements in mental health in treatment-seeking populations."[2]

Think of it this way: if someone is considering suicide, chances are that the conversation has happened so far only in the vacuum of their own thoughts. Being forced to discuss it out loud with another human being automatically reduces one of the most dangerous risk factors of all—*isolation.*

3. You are not responsible for the outcome.

The importance of this point cannot be overstated. Repeat it to yourself out loud if you must, but make sure you understand it before involving yourself in direct suicide intervention.

Why? Because it is not within your power to protect someone from a choice they are determined to make. Trying to do so can, in fact, work against effective intervention. More importantly, it can ultimately put *you* at risk in a couple of harmful ways. First, if you see yourself as someone's "savior," you are less likely to follow the guidelines below and may undertake unwise efforts in order to succeed. Second, in the event the person completes a suicide, you may be vulnerable to crippling feelings of guilt and failure that are totally unwarranted.

The Three C's of Alcoholics Anonymous advise how to handle a loved one's addiction: you didn't *cause* it, you can't *control* it, and you can't *cure* it. The same wisdom applies to suicide prevention as well.

4. Seek the help of trained professionals as soon as possible.

If you are involved in reaching out to someone in your life who is at risk of suicide, chances are good it's your first time in that role. You are as prepared as you can be—because you've cared enough to educate yourself—but there will always be a limit to your insight and experience, however well-intentioned you are. Remember to see yourself as a first responder whose job it is to stabilize a volatile situation, prevent immediate harm, and then enlist the help of people who do this sort of thing all day, every day. That doesn't mean your part is done—as we'll see in the steps below—only that you've had the wisdom to know where your expertise ends and someone else's begins.

Six Steps to Safety

As I said already, I consider these concrete actions in response to suicide risk to be practical and grounded in common sense. And yet, in a moment of crisis, those things are often the first to flee the scene. That's why it's important to take time to plan and prepare in advance, so that cooler heads—yours—can prevail. Write these steps down and place the list where you can refer to it as often as necessary to make it second nature when needed.

It's also worth noticing that while each step is vital on its own, they function as an integrated whole. You'll quickly see that it's necessary to practice them all in order to be truly effective. With all this in mind, here is what you can do to help someone in deep need.

1. Ask

The moment when someone's life may be at risk is not the time to subtly beat around the bush. Direct questions may not be easy, but in the case of suicide, research has shown they are an effective way to begin an intervention.

Don't be afraid to say, "Are you considering suicide right now?" One reason that's a powerful way to begin is it expects a yes or no answer while paving the way for lots of additional questions and conversation. If the reply is "yes," that's a clear invitation to go deeper into the reasons why. If "no," you've created an opportunity to explain what you've observed in them that made you ask the question in the first place—which may still lead to valuable connection.

Best of all, with such a bold and direct beginning, you've opened the door to follow with two of the most powerful questions of all—ones that break the barrier of isolation and create a connection that the person may not have felt in a long time:

"What is causing you pain?"

"How can I help?"

Suddenly, they are no longer alone because you cared enough to ask the tough questions.

100

SURVIVORS SPEAK:

SURVIVORS SPEAK:
A Timely Visit Saved Carmen from Despair

"I'd always heard the phrase 'saved by the bell,' but I had no idea what it really meant," Carmen told the gathered group of people who, like her, had survived their own suicide attempt. "Now I can say it literally happened to me."

Carmen was a painfully introverted teenager who had suffered from severe and untreated depression and anxiety her whole life. She compensated by overeating and, as a result, struggled with obesity on top of her mental challenges. These things combined to make her an easy and popular target for bullies at school.

"I'd had to deal with every kind of mean comment and prank for so long that I was convinced everyone was right about me and I deserved it all," she shared. "There was no reason to believe things would ever be different."

In other words, Carmen lived in a state of low-level misery and hopelessness all the time. Until one event pushed her over the edge into acute despair.

Someone took a photo of her eating a hot dog in the school cafeteria and modified it into a cruel meme with sexual implications. Then a number of kids posted it on social media. Carmen could only assume everyone had seen it.

"Looking at that I really got it, that the world would be a better place without me," she said. "And I'd be better off without the world."

At home alone that evening, Carmen found her mom's supply of powerful opioid painkillers, prescribed after a recent surgery. She also stole a bottle of whiskey from the liquor cabinet and went to her room. With the photo up on her computer, she downed a shot of the booze to calm her nerves and then emptied the pill bottle onto her desktop.

"I was going to take them all," she said. "Instead, I about jumped out of my skin when the doorbell rang. I was going to ignore it, but it rang again right away."

Annoyed, Carmen left her room and opened the door. Standing on the porch were three kids from her choir class—two girls and a boy.

"Lisa said something like, 'We just found out what happened. Are you okay?'" Carmen recalled. "And I lost it. I think about ten years' worth of hurt came flooding out."

Her visitors were part of a school initiative aimed at suicide prevention among young people. They'd participated in a recent weekend retreat to raise awareness of the problem and equip teens to notice and respond to distress among their peers.

"They stayed with me the whole night and made me call the hotline," Carmen said. "For the first time in my life someone said to me, 'You deserve so much better than this'—and I believed it."

Afterward, Carmen learned online that the term "saved by the bell" first appeared in an 1893 newspaper article to describe a boxer who was spared a knockout punch by the sound of the bell ending the round.

"If those people hadn't rung that bell, I think I really would have knocked myself all the way out."

2. Listen

Some lists only mention listening as part of the previous step of asking. But I believe it deserves its own place in the lineup because it is the crux of the matter, not an addendum. We've all had the experience of being asked a question by someone who then showed no interest in the answer or immediately took back the reins of the conversation, seeming to prefer their own answers to ours. In ordinary social settings, that's rude and annoying. In the context of a conversation about suicide, it should never happen.

However, it's far harder to be a good listener than we would like to think—especially in tense or uncomfortable situations—and therefore the topic deserves careful consideration. Here are two hypothetical scenarios that illustrate the problem:

"Are you thinking about killing yourself?"
"Yes."
"Oh my gosh, okay, here I'm dialing the hotline right now, and you need to . . ."

"What hurts you?"
"There's nothing left for me here. I don't believe my life will ever get better."
"But you're so wrong about that! You could . . ."

Not much listening or connecting going on there. These kinds of responses are well-intentioned but not very helpful when someone is in deep pain. Chances are one source of their isolation is that they don't feel they've ever been truly *heard*. So to give them that, consider:

A good listener isn't afraid of silence. Don't rush to fill every pause with comment. You are asking a person to share deep and difficult emotions. Give them plenty of space to do so.

A good listener leads the conversation with more questions, not commentary. Your purpose is to learn as much as you possibly can about your loved one's emotional and mental state. For example, a better path in the scenarios above would be to say, "Really? What makes you feel that way?" Or, "I know that you're hurting. Can you tell me more about what you're thinking and feeling?"

Furthermore, you want to discover where they are in their journey toward suicide—early ideation or advanced planning? Have they already acquired the lethal means to complete a suicide? You'll never gain this information if you do the talking.

A good listener doesn't judge what they hear. A person who admits to considering suicide expects to be condemned for it.

Surprise them with acceptance, understanding, and empathy. That will make them more likely to open up and share their real feelings—a critical step in successful intervention.

Mastering the skill of listening takes practice. Start now and watch all your relationships benefit!

3. Be there

We've seen it again and again throughout this book—and in volumes of research on the subject of suicide: social isolation can be the most lethal condition of all for someone who has succumbed to hopelessness and despair.

However, that points to an obvious and readily available remedy—*connectedness.* While this usually is meant to address the general condition of a person's life, it takes on increased power and relevance in moments of acute crisis. Having someone who is committed to being present in a time of need—whether being present in person, by phone, online, or with frequent texts—has been shown to decrease suicide risk.[3]

4. Do what you can to keep them safe

If you've asked all the tough questions and really listened to the answers, you now have a good idea of how imminent and severe the person's risk of suicide is. You know, for example, if they are already in possession of lethal means—a firearm, medications, and so on. You've assessed their state of mind, including their present level of intoxication or impairment.

This step is about taking action to *limit their access* to those things and slow the process down, allowing them more time to think. Here's an important caveat: *this should never involve putting yourself at risk.* For example, if you believe the person has a firearm and is serious about using it, or if they become aggressive or violent at any time, call the authorities! Remember, the goal is not to take full responsibility yourself but to choose the best way possible to protect the at-risk person—and yourself.

While a lot of attention has been paid to understanding *why* people commit suicide, a growing number of studies also focus on the importance of *how* in order to shape sound intervention tactics. One interesting finding—with direct bearing on the importance of this step—reveals how quickly many people reach for available lethal means once they've decided to kill themselves. "While some suicides are deliberative and involve careful planning, many appear to have been hastily decided-upon and to involve little or no planning. Chronic, underlying risk factors such as substance abuse and depression are also often present, but the acute period of heightened risk for suicidal behavior is often only minutes or hours long."[4]

Here are results of a recent survey of 153 suicide survivors asking how much time elapsed between forming the intention to commit suicide and actually making an attempt:

- 24 percent said less than 5 minutes
- 24 percent said 5–19 minutes
- 23 percent said 20 minutes to 1 hour
- 16 percent said 2–8 hours
- 13 percent said 1 or more days[5]

One in four said less than five minutes went by—illustrating how important it can be to limit access to lethal means as soon as possible.

5. Help them find professional assistance

The value in this step is multidimensional—first, in the moment of acute crisis, through talking with a trained and experienced counselor at one of the National Suicide Prevention Lifeline's crisis hotlines. People who answer those phones have all received what's known as Applied Suicide Intervention Skills Training (ASIST). One analysis of the program's effectiveness reported, "Callers were significantly more likely to feel less depressed, less suicidal, less overwhelmed, and more hopeful by the end of calls handled by ASIST-trained counselors."[6]

Second, access to professional care is critical for a person's long-term recovery and well-being. As we've seen, untreated or poorly regulated mental health disorders play an enormous role in suicide risk. Steering a person toward the care they need can not only defuse an immediate suicide threat, but also make all the difference in eliminating it for good.

6. Follow up

Research has shown that when hotlines and emergency care providers make follow-up contact within twenty-four to forty-eight hours with someone in a suicide ideation crisis, the chances of recurrence are drastically reduced.[7]

If that's true for professional relationships, imagine how much more powerful follow-up may be from someone the person knows and loves. These days, making contact with someone has never been easier:

- Call on the phone
- Send a text
- Write a letter or send a postcard
- Visit in person
- Deliver a small gift
- Enlist others to do the same

Maintain the connection you established in moments of crisis and you'll do more than simply avert one tragic outcome—you'll help save a life for good.

Hope Renewed, Life Restored

There is a thread that winds its way through all the above and binds them together. Offering a lifeline to someone suffering great pain is not a by-the-numbers exercise, but an expression of the most powerful force on earth: *love.*

> Love is patient, love is kind. It does not envy, it does not boast, it is not proud. It does not dishonor others, it is not self-seeking, it is not easily angered, it keeps no record of wrongs. Love does not delight in evil but rejoices with the truth. It always protects, always trusts, always hopes, always perseveres. (1 Cor. 13:4–7)

Let this kind of love be your guide—backed by your own faith in God and hope in his healing grace—and you'll be an effective voice of comfort and refuge when someone needs you most.

—9—

Whole-Person Wellness

Solid Steps toward Stability

For many months, Mitchell had struggled with feelings of deep depression, lack of energy, and low self-esteem. His poor physical health and lifestyle habits contributed greatly to his poor mental health. Mitchell slept poorly almost every night, ate little except for comfort food, and spent countless hours aimlessly surfing the internet. Admittedly, he felt either angry or numb about issues at work or life in general. He felt worthless and hopeless and saw little reason to keep trying at life and had contemplated suicide more than once.

Using the whole-person approach, my team and I counseled Mitchell on multiple fronts. A first-step strategy we used with him turned out to be a powerful one: we worked with him to improve the quality of his sleep. This may seem like an obvious place to start, but I am continually amazed at how many people don't sleep well and don't do anything to change the disruptive patterns.

I gave Mitchell a "prescription" to create a healthy evening routine and to keep a sleep log, in which he could write down exactly what he did, watched, and consumed each night prior to bedtime. As we reviewed his routine over several weeks, he realized a number of habits that were contributing to his poor sleep: he consistently took his smartphone into bed with him, sending texts and checking social media sites right before turning out the light; he consumed a drink or two of alcohol close to bedtime; and he usually kept the TV on in his bedroom as background noise.

It took discipline and intentional choices to change his routine. But over time, Mitchell gradually adopted habits that facilitated good sleep, rather than undermined it. Eventually, he began sleeping more—and sleeping more deeply—each night.

For Mitchell, recognizing unproductive habits and improving his sleep hygiene represented a solid step in the right direction—a positive and practical step on his journey through depression and suicidal thoughts. He would go on to work through many issues related to lifestyle routines and practices.

With the help of a counselor, a nutritionist, and other members of the team at our clinic, Mitchell learned how much he had been affected by not only insomnia but also poor eating habits, excessive drinking, and little exercise. A lack of consistent healthy habits contributed significantly to his chronic depression, which sometimes led him to believe that life wasn't worth living and to even contemplate ways he could end his life.

There are no magic formulas for overcoming mental health struggles—no easy-to-follow plan that will provide instant healing for a person's emotional troubles. However, I am convinced of the life-changing power of committing to specific actions and attitudes that promote physical, emotional, spiritual, and mental health.

Did Mitchell's intentional plan to improve his sleep cause his depression (and suicidal thoughts) to completely go away? No, of course not. There were other important issues he needed to address with the help of professionals. But achieving consistent, quality sleep was a significant component in his recovery and well-being. Taken individually, these steps—sleep, nutrition, exercise, and so on—may seem like small steps forward, but taken together they create a huge leap toward strength and wholeness.

A Prime Example of Whole-Person Health

A verse in Scripture beautifully summarizes the growing-up years of Jesus: "And Jesus increased in wisdom and stature, and in favor with God and men" (Luke 2:52 NKJV). This succinct statement underscores how Jesus lived his life in balance, even during his formative years, paying attention to his mental, physical, spiritual, and social-emotional development. This well-rounded approach helped prepare and strengthen him for a ministry that would change the world and serve as a role model for millions of people down through the ages.

Luke's portrait of Christ's healthy development entails four major areas of life that God has breathed into every one of us. He gave us a mind to think with and to exercise wisdom; a spirit with the capacity for relationship with God; emotions to express joy and sorrow, which are often closely linked to our social well-being; and a body to house it all, circulate life-giving blood, and experience pain and pleasure through thousands of nerves. He designed us to enjoy the optimal performance and functionality that happens when all of these components are healthfully integrated.

In John 10:10, Jesus called this the "abundant" life—living life to the full, according to God's design. When we are fully engaged in pursuing mental, physical, spiritual, and emotional-relational peace, Jesus assures us that he came "that they may have life, and . . . have it more abundantly" (NKJV).

God wants us to be whole.

This is why, at our clinic, we apply the whole-person approach to our clients' mental and emotional challenges. We have found that if a person is deficient in one or two of these key areas of life, it usually has a harmful effect on the other areas—and on the whole person. When your body doesn't feel well, your thought life, spiritual life, and emotional life may also suffer. When your emotions are frayed, your body, mind, and spirit may feel depleted as well.

So it follows that, as we have found at The Center, effective healing is more likely when we treat the *whole person* and not just their immediate, presenting symptoms. And this is especially true when working with suicidal or post-suicidal clients. More than ever before, they need whole-person wellness.

Finding Sustainable Progress

If you have played a role in helping prevent a friend from taking their life, it's important to know that the battle is not over. In previous chapters we viewed sad statistics detailing the percentage of suicidal men and women who later try again. Many of the factors contributing to suicidal ideation that we've examined in these chapters do not diminish with the mere passage of time—they are persistent issues that are likely to revisit.

That's why I am presenting this information here: to help you help your loved one move beyond the suicidal spiral and pursue balanced, whole-person healing. You'll want to talk through these components with your loved one and, as much as you can, ensure that they are following these wellness strategies in collaboration with their medical and mental health professionals. Consider active participation whenever you can, such as partnering for healthier nutrition and exercise. It will be good for you too!

A Strong Body

As we seek to build whole-person wellness, it is essential to start by getting the body healthy and strong. Why? Because the body, mind, spirit, and emotions are so interdependent that they affect one another, for better or worse. As theologian-educator Anthony

Coniaris observes, "The truth is that the body and the soul live so close to each other that they often catch one another's sicknesses, illnesses, and diseases."[1] Since an unsound body can be a gateway to all sorts of mental, spiritual, and emotional challenges, we'll focus first on physical health.

Check Your Fuel

Our bodies require proper fuel in order to supply the brain with the nutrients it needs to calmly process inputs and generate rational thought. But in the face of this need, we tend to consume too many unhealthy foods and too few healthy ones.

To help conquer the sluggishness and negative emotions that spiraled your friend to suicidal tendencies, they need intentional improvement in the fuel they feed their body.

Water. We need water, and large amounts of it, throughout the day for our organs, skin, and blood to function properly. Even mild dehydration can make us feel weak and pull down our mood. The adult human body is 50 to 65 percent water, and the blood that courses through our arteries and veins is 92 percent water. This blood supplies the muscles, nervous system, heart, and brain with the oxygen and nutrients they need. So start each day with sixteen ounces of water and try to consume this amount at least four or five more times throughout the day, easing off a few hours before bedtime.

Fresh produce. Each and every day, the human body needs multiple servings of fresh fruit and fresh vegetables for the life-giving nutrients they offer. Recent studies have determined that we should try to consume a total of *nine* moderate servings of fresh fruit and vegetables with our meals and as snacks throughout the day.

Whole-grain foods. Building a healthy body also requires whole-grain foods. Cut back (*way* back) on highly processed, nutrition-free chips, packaged snacks, white breads, and sugared cereals. Discover the great taste and energy boost of whole-grain breads with organic almond butter, or steel-cut oatmeal or unsweetened granola with fresh berries.

Lean meats and fish, eggs, nuts, low-fat dairy. Deep-fried meats or fish should be minimized; grilled or baked is far healthier. Fish and fish oil provide healthy fats, as do unprocessed nuts and seeds such as raw almonds, walnuts, and sunflower seeds. If you have trouble digesting milk, you'll want to consider lactose-free products such as almond milk.

Nutritional supplements. Few of us have the time or inclination to figure out all the food combinations we would need to make sure we get enough selenium, calcium, magnesium, and zinc, to say nothing of all the vitamins, minerals, and micronutrients our bodies require. A quality nutritional supplement conveniently ensures that we receive the balanced nutrition that even a healthy diet may lack.

Limit coffee and energy drinks. It seems we're a culture addicted to caffeine, which increases the heart rate and blood pressure and makes you jittery and nervous, compounding the downward spiral. Encourage your loved one to ease off the caffeine habit by cutting daily consumption to just one or two cups of coffee with a healthy protein breakfast in the morning, and avoid those highly sugared, highly caffeinated so-called energy drinks altogether.

Stay away from sweet treats. Refined sugar can make blood glucose levels spike, then rapidly plummet, which only exacerbates the negative physical and emotional downswings we're working so hard to overcome. Avoiding dramatic ups and downs in blood glucose levels will help your friend stabilize their mood, calm their system, and improve their overall energy. Again, with sweet treats (or any foods or drinks with added sugar) moderation is the key, and only after a healthy meal.

Get Moving

Scientists have found that regular, moderate exercise decreases overall levels of tension, elevates and stabilizes mood, improves sleep quality, and improves self-esteem. Why? Because exercise increases the release of essential chemicals and hormones that have a major impact on brain health and mood. These chemicals include *serotonin*, a natural mood stabilizer essential in combatting depression; *norepinephrine*, which affects alertness, focus, and memory; *dopamine*, a neurotransmitter linked to pleasure and motivation; and *endorphins*—often called "feel-good" chemicals because they can act as a pain reliever and happiness booster.

And those are just the mood-stabilizing benefits. Regular exercise also enhances muscular and cardiovascular fitness, which boosts overall physical strength and endurance. All of these benefits help fortify a struggler's self-confidence and ability to fight the downward pull.

Start simply, but start now. With your friend, challenge each other to park farther out from the workplace entrance or grocery store. Take stairs instead of elevators or escalators. Replace "coffee breaks" with brief walks—outside whenever weather permits. Designate specific times and places where you'll meet to exercise together, then follow through.

Get Quality ZZZs

I told you about my client Mitchell's trouble with sleeping well, and maybe you can relate. When you don't get enough sleep, your body, brain, and emotions suffer, and you experience undesirable symptoms such as:

- Decreased overall activity in the brain, which impacts focus, learning, memory, and productivity
- Impaired driving alertness and response times
- Interference with healthy heart function
- Compromises in how your body repairs joint and muscle injuries

115

- A "shorter fuse," meaning that your usual mental and emotional filters are compromised and you feel crabby and irritable, less able to respond patiently and diplomatically to the day's challenges
- Increased tendencies toward discouragement, diminishment, and depression
- Lessened physical, mental, and emotional strength to overcome suicidal ideation

Healthy nutrition and consistent exercise are great for helping induce restorative sleep. So are a warm bath, reading the Bible or other tranquil reading, and prayer. I recommend that you halt screen time (TV, phones, tablets) at least one hour prior to bed, because continued exposure to electronic media increases anxious or demoralizing thoughts at a time when your mind needs peace.

Keep your bedroom cool and dark. After you tuck in, breathe deeply and slowly, inhaling through your nose and exhaling through your mouth. No matter what took place during the day, now's the time to "cast all your anxiety on [the Lord] because he cares for you" (1 Pet. 5:7). Now's also the time to think of at least three blessings for which you're grateful—and to thank God for them as you breathe deeply.

I can't emphasize enough the importance of sound physical health for both the caregiver and the troubled friend or family member. As you and your friend work together toward healthier physical habits, you'll discover greater levels of mental, emotional, and spiritual strength to help cope with the stresses and discouragements of life.

A Sound Mind

Disappointment, discouragement, diminishment, depression, and despair are all fueled by our thoughts—and by the way we choose to *feel* about our thoughts.

116

It takes sound thoughts, from a sound mind, to develop sound feelings or a reliable emotional response. Likewise, unstable thoughts can lead to unstable feelings or unreliable emotional responses. So it's crucial that you encourage your friend to maintain a strong mind and a healthy thought life on the journey to stability. For our purposes in this chapter, let's focus on the all-important shift from a negative outlook to a positive one.

An upbeat, positive outlook is a key ingredient for mental health as well as whole-person balance. Not only is an upbeat person far more pleasant to be around, but they will also enjoy a much greater level of inner peace and contentment.

A positive perspective better equips a struggler to fend off the initial stages of the deadly downward spiral—by not letting disappointments seem so devastating or overthinking them into discouragement, diminishment, or depression.

Could this be why Proverbs 23:7 (NKJV) tells us, "For as [a man] thinks in his heart, so is he"? It's so true that as we think, we are. If we dwell on defeated thoughts, we live in defeat. But if we think upbeat, cheerful thoughts, we're upbeat, cheerful people— and life's difficulties are much less prone to take hold and bring us down.

But can a person who isn't naturally upbeat develop a positive outlook? Absolutely. Optimism isn't just something a person is born with; it can be learned and exercised, like a muscle. And you can help your friend do just that.

A positive outlook is, at its core, a way of reframing an obstacle or a potentially upsetting input. Take a quick inventory of your own inner voice. Do thoughts like these sound at all familiar?

- *Why bother? I'll never lose weight.*
- *They just don't like me.*
- *Knowing me, I'll just blow it.*

- *Can't I ever catch a break?*
- *I'm so stupid.*
- *They don't value my opinion, so why speak up?*

If you find that your thinking tends to default toward the negative, your inner voice could use a tune-up. And, thankfully, we can reduce discouragement by changing our internal conversation.

A good place to start is by reviewing those "7 Powerful Promises" from the Scriptures that I suggested you memorize back in chapter 7. Go over these again, thanking God for each promise and claiming it as your personal promise from him. He cares about you, and he cares how you think and talk to yourself!

Here are some other alternatives to help you reject dismal self-talk and respond to any situation more confidently:

- *Of course I can do this. I've succeeded at many things before.*
- *Maybe he was just having a hard day.*
- *What's good about this? What can I learn from it?*
- *One bad moment does not make a bad day.*
- *Tomorrow's a new day.*
- *God loves me just as I am, even with my shortcomings.*
- *It'll look better in the morning.*

Be kind to yourself. Speak kindly to yourself and about others. Many strugglers see a significant reduction in disappointment, discouragement, diminishment, or depression when they learn to address themselves with more compassion.

You are not a slave to pessimistic, dispirited thinking. It is within your power to control and shape your thoughts to be calm, confident, and life-giving. You can indeed approach and respond to life with a healthy perspective!

Give Life the Benefit of the Doubt

An observant friend remembers that while Janice had a soft laugh, her smile would often evaporate quickly as she seemed to withdraw into some kind of private sorrow.

Counselors and family wouldn't learn until later that, in her preteen years, Janice had been repeatedly touched inappropriately by an acquaintance of her older brother. It had left her unnerved and confused—especially after the older boy mocked her for being frightened and then threatened to tell "all the boys" that she enjoyed it and had "asked for it."

In the years that followed, Janice grew more withdrawn and less trusting. Eye contact was difficult for her. Those closest to her noticed that her eyes always seemed filled with sadness and often on the verge of tears.

"Looking back, I had little self-confidence," Janice recalls. "I had no faith in myself and very little faith in others. My whole outlook became cynical and negative. I know now that it was depression."

Janice describes the feeling as "no energy, no capability of excitement, continually numb." She found herself assuming the worst about everyone and everything. Her depression caused her to withdraw further because, as she says, "I didn't want to be around anyone. I didn't think anyone would want to be around me. I didn't think anyone understood or cared."

The sad suicide attempt came one weekday evening, after a particularly disheartening day at her job. Feeling hopeless and spent, she popped the lid from her sleep medication and shook out the remaining eight tablets. Was it enough to put her to sleep permanently? She didn't know. Did she really want to do this? She didn't know. But she so wanted to escape the relentless, lonely despair of feeling like a nobody. She swallowed the pills and chased the meds with water. Then she picked up her cell phone and texted a friend: *Finally I've taken control.*

Fortunately, her friend knew of Janice's struggles and read between the lines. The friend hurried to Janice's house and got to her in time, calling 9-1-1 immediately.

In counseling since then, Janice has been working with her therapist on multiple fronts. "One of the things my counselor is teaching me," she says, "is to redirect my thoughts and remarks away from pessimism and toward the positive. I'm trying to practice deliberate, intentional gratitude."

She continues: "I'm keeping a gratitude journal, where I write down at least three things each day that I'm thankful for. We do exercises in which I have to deliberately shift from a negative perspective to a positive one. For example, if I'm thinking, *My job sucks,* she challenges me to recast my negativity into a blessing to be grateful for, such as *I'm so grateful for a job to go to each day.*"

It takes practice, but along with the rest of her therapy, Janice is gradually retraining her mind to default to the positive. By taking initiative to express gratitude, she is realizing that the world is not against her and life holds a multitude of blessings to be thankful for. An "attitude of gratitude" has become a powerful tool in her toolbox.

Social-Emotional Strength

As we've seen, what we think about a situation leads to our feelings about that situation. Our emotions may take just a fraction of a second or they may start small and build up over time, but our emotions tend to amplify whatever it is we're thinking.

If a person says something you perceive as insulting, your perception is what you think: *Wow, that was snarky.* The nature of your thought then generates your emotional response: *What an insult! That really hurt!* Your perception becomes visceral in the form of a negative emotion.

Just as negative thoughts lead to negative emotions, positive thoughts lead to positive emotions and, by extension, better overall emotional health. In the example above, let's say you've committed to think the best of people instead of the worst. When someone makes what could be interpreted as a snarky remark, you choose to think instead, *Okay, this person is having a tough day.* This more cheerful perception gives people the benefit of the doubt and removes hurtful snark from the equation. Your emotional response is then more likely to be compassionate, such as, *I'll ask them if there's anything I can do to help today.*

Lighten Up—on Yourself and on Others

A key reason we may experience runaway emotions is that we try to live up to unrealistic standards—and we expect others to do the same. People are fallible, yourself included. Yet God loves us anyway and doesn't hold our failings against us. You'll take a major step toward healing and stability by following his lead and lightening up on yourself and others. Give yourself, others, and life's circumstances the benefit of the doubt, and resolve to not take perceived offenses so seriously. Jesus taught forgiveness, so forgive and ask forgiveness.

Commit to thinking the best of others instead of the worst, and you'll be much more likely to find and enjoy life's blessings instead of the drawbacks. Which goes a long way toward emotional healing.

Continue Professional Help

As your friend continues the journey to stability, it's crucial that they continue getting regular professional help through counseling. Talk therapies can be especially helpful. At The Center we use a form of talk therapy called dialectical behavioral therapy (DBT), which is a clear and cogent process for working through strong emotions and shifting them from harmful to helpful. Using these techniques or others, a compassionate counselor can show your friend all the ways their emotions have turned into maladapted behaviors—and equip them to exchange negative responses for constructive ones. With God's help and your encouragement, your friend can learn to choose the healthier path.

Strong in Spirit

As you probably know by now, I am confidently up-front about my faith in God. I never pressure acquaintances, clients, readers, or audiences to believe as I do, but I embrace the Christian faith as revealed in the Scriptures and have found it to be an incredible source of strength and guidance in all aspects of my life, personal and professional.

I like the way Blaise Pascal described our spiritual dimension: a *God-shaped vacuum.* In a quote commonly attributed to the French physicist-philosopher, he says, "There is a God-shaped vacuum in the heart of each man which cannot be filled by any created thing, but only by God, the Creator, made known through Jesus Christ." In other words, every one of us has a place in our spirit that longs for knowledge and intimacy with God our Creator.

But whether from unbelief or self-reliance, we try very hard to fill the God-shaped vacuum with other things we think will satisfy—career, money, friends, activity, sports, sex, food, cars, good works . . . and enough stuff to fill our garages, basements, and rented storage spaces to overflowing. But do these things truly fill the spiritual vacuum? Or will they ultimately cause us to lament, in the words of Peggy Lee's 1969 classic song, "Is that all there is?"

Consider the wisest and richest king of his time.

A Wise Man's Errant Journey

As a young king, Solomon believed that trusting in God and seeking his guidance was the path to wisdom and success. And as long as Solomon lived by his faith in God, he was richly and wonderfully blessed. We often speak of "the wisdom of Solomon." But his journey is actually a cautionary tale.

Sadly, as Solomon acquired more and more wives, concubines, wealth, gold, and "stuff," he drifted from his faith. Later, as he looked back on his life with deep regrets, he called all of his acquisitions and activities and possessions "meaningless" (Eccles. 1:2)—his way of saying, "Is that all there is?" He longed for the days of intimacy with his Creator. He'd tried filling the God-shaped vacuum with the stuff of this world, and he knew better all along.

I don't want you or your friend to make the mistake Solomon made. By filling the God-shaped vacuum with God instead of stuff, you'll find that soul care through faith is an empowering new way of life. Jesus taught and modeled love and joy, peace and grace, compassion and forgiveness. Following his teachings works hand in hand with everything else you're learning in this book, and the result can be life-changing, giving us the strength to move confidently toward wholeness and stability.

But it takes a daily, moment-by-moment commitment. No Solomon-like caving to the culture. To help your friend enjoy a more personal and powerful spiritual dimension, encourage them to engage in enriching practices such as these:

Talk with God Early and Often

Jesus told his followers, "For everyone who asks receives; the one who seeks finds; and to the one who knocks, the door will be opened" (Matt. 7:8). God actually *invites* us to seek his help, strength, and wisdom in the daily battles we face. Your prayer needn't be formal or fancy, just honest. God longs to hear from the real you—as early and as often as you want to talk with him. Tell him how you're feeling, what you're struggling with. Ask him for physical strength, mental and emotional toughness, and wisdom. Cast your cares upon him, because he cares for you.

Read the Bible and Other Sacred Texts

The history of humanity is one long search for meaning and connection to our origins and true nature. Fortunately, there is a written record of the quest. Poets and mystics of all kinds have littered the road with bread crumbs leading us back to ourselves—and to a loving, nurturing, healing God. I especially recommend the Holy Bible—perhaps starting with the Psalms, or Paul's letter to the Philippians, or the Gospel of John. You may wish to try a modern paraphrase such as the New Living Translation or *The Message*. Feel free to mark it up, underscoring and memorizing key verses that are especially meaningful to you.

Guard Your Thoughts

Each of us has a cacophony of messages continually fighting for our attention. Some are good, many are bad. But as we saw earlier in this chapter, it's within your power to choose which thoughts and ideas you will feed and which you will let starve. It comes down to our self-talk, which can either empower us or defeat us. Commit to choosing healthy thoughts like the ones we've suggested in this book:

- Scriptural promises that focus on God's love and presence
- Favorable thoughts that give others the benefit of the doubt
- Responses that *forgive* those who've offended you and *ask forgiveness* when you've offended others
- Upbeat responses that *look for the good* in life's twists and turns

Today is a new day. Nurture the helpful, healing thoughts and banish the ones that pull you down.

Dwell in an Attitude of Gratitude

Gratitude is a matter not only of the mind but also of the spirit. Yet many people overlook life's many blessings or can't acknowledge the good when they feel so bad. Make the deliberate choice

124

each day to be grateful. On a walk with a friend, observe and mention things you're grateful for: a beautiful wildflower, the cloud formations in the sky, a funny squirrel, or a bird's happy song. Keep a gratitude journal and review it often. Before sleep, think of at least three blessings—large or small—that came your way during the day. Thank God for them.

And . . . be grateful that he is strengthening and guiding your journey to healing, stability, and wholeness. Indeed, there is hope, and there is so much to live for.

—10—

Learning to Live Again

Helpful Steps toward a Hopeful Future

Tomorrow will be much better than yesterday.

Next week will be much better than last week.

Next year will be much better than last year.

That is the message people struggling with suicidal thoughts need to hear and need to believe.

As you seek to help the loved one you're concerned about, strive to impart this point: though life has been extremely painful in the past and continues to be painful at the present moment, the future can be so much better and brighter.

An extraordinary future is available to anyone—to you and the person you're seeking to encourage. All people can be free to grow, enjoy meaningful relationships, have adventures, pursue ambitions, and experience new reasons to love life. In other words, everyone can be empowered to live a life of abundance, fulfillment, and contentment.

As you come alongside the struggling person you are close to, emphasize the steps discussed in this chapter as helpful ways to move toward a hope-filled future.

Replenish Your Emotional Energy

For the vast majority of people, life is hectic, stressful, and exhausting. With pressure at work, weekend obligations, household chores, kids and/or parents to care for, who has time for rest and renewal?

One of our society's most irrational ideas is that we should always push the limits. Maximize your busyness, speed, and efficiency—then increase it another 10 percent! While this approach makes us feel productive, it is hard on our emotional lives. In every area of your life, seek to create reserves—a buffer against the things that deplete you. Allow extra time to complete a project. Spend less than you earn. Get rid of some possessions rather than acquiring more.

Since all of us are created uniquely, we each have different ways to rejuvenate ourselves. Extroverts get recharged by being around other people. Introverts get recharged by walking quietly in the woods or curling up with a good book. Creative people may need to regularly attend the symphony or explore an art gallery. Nature lovers need to go hiking or work in the garden. Identify your boosters and employ them often.

Keep this in mind too: Life is full of people, obligations, and tasks that siphon off our energy. Some we can't avoid—but some we can and should. Cut back on car trips that leave you stuck in traffic. Steer clear of people who soak up your energy like a dry sponge in a puddle of water.

Revive Your Purpose

Many people hear the word *purpose* and think it applies only to epic, world-changing work. Not so. I define purpose as the *one unique thing* we each have to offer the world, no matter how big or small. Its absence might not make headlines, but it absolutely would be missed by those who stand to benefit from your gifts.

Your personal purpose may be to pour all your energy and creativity into raising healthy children; to teach watercolor painting to residents in a retirement center; to be the most caring and conscientious insurance agent your clients have ever known; or to teach preschool in a way that endows kids with self-respect and self-confidence. The list of possibilities is long. Only you can know which one best describes you.

Here's the secret to finding your purpose: Start by creating a list of things you have loved doing in your life. Chances are, what you're meant to do now is something you couldn't stop doing as a younger person but that you abandoned somewhere along the way. Or it may be the thing you still didn't dare put on the list but that tugs at your sleeve anyway.

Why is finding and following your purpose so important when revitalizing your future? Because it's what gets you out of bed on a dreary Monday morning in the middle of winter. Purpose is your answer to the question why. Why keep a grip on my addictive impulses? Why watch what I eat? Why care about toxic emotions and their effect on my health and well-being? Why guard against old habits?

Because you have a purpose, a role to play in the lives of others. Those others may be abandoned animals at the local shelter or everyone who looks at a piece of your art and is inspired or moved. It may be cliché these days, but it's never been more true: the world needs *everyone* to fulfill their purpose—you included.

Reset Your Pace

In order to maintain a balanced pace of life, you need to "stop the car" and get your obligations under control. You may have invited them along for the ride, but you're still the driver of the car. You can tell some of them to take a hike or, at least, get in the back and stop trying to take the wheel away from you.

Did you notice I said to stop the car? Some people are afraid to do so. To stop moving means risking the collective weight of all of their obligations piling up and crushing them. They are convinced that to remain safe, they must stay one step ahead of their obligations. Outrunning is safe; stopping spells disaster.

Stop and take stock of your priorities and your obligations. Stop and examine where and how you spend your time. Stop and determine what is actually necessary. Stop and carve out time for thought and reflection. Many people rarely give themselves permission to stop and reevaluate their activity, resenting anything that hinders forward motion.

Actions, as they say, speak louder than words. People act either to create something they desire or to avoid something they fear. What do your actions say about what you desire and what you fear? These are your true priorities.

What happens to gears that are out of alignment? They grind and grate and scrape against each other; gears out of alignment create damage. Compare and contrast what you want your priorities to be and what your priorities are. The more out of alignment these are, the more you live at odds with yourself. The more you live at odds with yourself, the more stress you'll have in your life.

Resetting your pace may seem like an exercise in reducing the amount of things you do and thus only applicable to hard-charging, type-A people. Simplifying your life, however, is about making sure the things you do provide meaning and positive purpose in your life.

Emotional distress is created not merely by doing too many things; it is also created by doing too many of the wrong things and not enough of the right things. Looking at your life through that filter can help you determine what you need to keep and what things you need to let go.

Life is about choices. Each yes and each no reveal something about who you are as a person. You can't start to change until you understand who you are. Once you understand who you are, you are better able to bring yourself into alignment with who God wants you to be and how he wants you to live your life. God does not want you to live so weighed down by obligations that you miss out on life.

Reconnect with Trusted People

Healing from heartache almost always happens with the support and care of other people. Relationships are a crucial part of life—especially for those seeking to achieve emotional wellness.

According to information provided by the American Psychological Association, numerous studies continue to suggest that not only does social isolation rob you of help others have to give, but it has serious physical and mental consequences in itself—including an elevated risk of anxiety and depression.[1]

Therefore, it's important to evaluate the relationships in your life to weed out any toxic relationships and also determine if you have enough relational support around you.

Here are several qualities that are essential for strong, healthy relationships.

Trust. Friends trust each other because each has proven to be trustworthy. When tempted to betray the friendship in some way, they have held fast to the needs and feelings of the other person.

Honesty. One of the hallmarks of true friendship is living within an atmosphere of truth. This truth, however, is not a harsh, brutal presentation but one done in love, compassion, and tenderness. To a friend, the truth is not a weapon—it is a balm. There is safety in the honest words of a friend, even when those words hurt.

Understanding. True friends understand each other. They know the background and context of each other's lives. They know the *what* of things, but they also know the *why* of things. Friends know which way the other will jump and how far.

Acceptance. Healthy people understand the precarious positions they put themselves in by being a friend. Proximity sometimes equates to pain where human beings are concerned; friends acknowledge this pain as an acceptable consequence of the friendship.

Sacrifice. There are times when friendship calls for sacrifice. It can be a sacrifice of time, money, energy, resources—a reordering of priorities to put the needs of friendship first.

Affection. At the heart of all friendships should be genuine affection one for the other. Friends enjoy each other; they like being together because of the way they feel about each other.

This is not to say you should discount any relationship that does not live up to these standards. It is simply a means of putting such a relationship in perspective. Especially during times of difficulty, it is important to have a support system of friends around you.

If you want to become emotionally healthy, surround yourself with healthy people.

Recalibrate Your Perspective

Your life patterns and choices are the result of your perception of life and what you believed would happen. These are often forged in childhood. Once you understand your personal life patterns, you will be better able to discover certain perceptions and expectations that led you to either negative or positive actions.

If your life patterns are framed in negativity, you can be sure your perceptions and expectations were also negative. The more negative your perceptions and expectations become, the greater they support any negative life patterns.

You may think of perceptions as your filters through which you view the events of your life. Some people who seem perennially happy are considered to view life through "rose-colored glasses." Their filters are weighted on the side of the positive. Those who struggle with depression view life through "gray-colored glasses." Life appears negative, oppressive, and filled with problems.

To overcome depression and move toward wellness, you may need to change the way you view life. If you believe life consistently treats you unfairly, then the inevitable ups and downs of life are filtered through that perception. Up times seem imaginary and are

SURVIVORS SPEAK:
Tanya's Tragedy Culminated in Triumph

A decade ago, Tanya's oldest child, Dylan, then seventeen years old, began to display unusual behavior. For Tanya—who worked with teenagers every day as a youth pastor at a Dallas church—signs began to appear that all was not right with her son. All his life, Dylan had been well known among friends and family as an outgoing, thoughtful, and generous kid. But he had become noticeably withdrawn and angry. Numerous people mentioned to Tanya that "something has changed" with Dylan, and he didn't seem like his typical charming, carefree self.

Tanya discovered that Dylan had been sinking deeper into drug and alcohol use, which contributed to his frequent mood swings and erratic behavior. Over time, he became obsessed with conspiracy theories and made alarming statements about people being "out to get me."

Through a series of troubling incidents, medical evaluations, and hospitalizations, Dylan's physicians diagnosed him with bipolar disorder, which was complicated by his ADHD. Over the coming year, Dylan experienced a descent into deep depression. More treatment, medication, and assistance followed—with family members and specialists doing all they could to help. Tragically, however, these interventions were not enough. In October 2011, Dylan took his own life at age eighteen.

The tragic loss left Tanya, her family, and their entire community devastated and heartbroken. Tanya faced the question of how to move on amid heartache and sorrow.

To allow herself time to heal and care for her family, Tanya left her youth pastor position and, after an extended time away, began volunteering at a senior-citizens center and with rescue dogs awaiting adoption. In time, she added to her volunteer endeavors a day per week assisting at-risk high school kids in jeopardy of dropping out.

"I learned that the saying is true: giving to others is the best way to give to yourself."

These service opportunities, she said, helped her healing process—and also helped her find her next vocational step as a guidance counselor at a continuation school, now helping students stay in school and earn a diploma.

"I found a new calling that utilized my experience as a youth pastor and also my personal tragedy to help others," she recalls. "Students transferring to a continuation school are troubled and fragile because of stress, family crises, poverty, or mental health challenges. They're just trying to navigate high school and life."

Because of her own pain and hardship, Tanya brings exceptional empathy and understanding to the students she interacts with. Working with several hundred students each year, Tanya serves as a combination guidance counselor, academic coach, advocate, listening ear, encourager, and sometimes surrogate mom. She is heavily invested in giving these kids life experiences otherwise not available to them, such as excursions to the theater and museums, often paying out of her own pocket. Through countless hours spent with these teenagers, Tanya is concerned about their academic success but even more so about their emotional well-being.

"I've been a counselor for several years now, and I feel so grateful to have a career that draws on my life experiences to help guide, support, and nurture young people. Because of my son's difficulties and because he died by suicide, I am especially attuned to the challenges teenagers face. And I watch carefully for signs that they are depressed and perhaps suicidal."

enjoyed with suspicion, if at all, while times of disappointment are considered normal or par for the course.

If you have the perception that your life is supposed to always be smooth sailing, the inevitable downs can cause great anxiety. Down times can be put into proper perspective when you regard them as a part of life but don't feel dominated by them. Problems and disappointments happen, of course, but you won't be weighed down by them for long.

Conversely, if you are unprepared to deal with these down times, confusion, frustration, and depression can result. If you have the perception that you don't deserve to be happy, you will filter the events of your life to make sure you aren't content. If you have the perception that the only way for you to be safe is to be in control, you will have a heightened sense of anxiety over life events. Since people are rarely in total control of their environment, and never in control of other people, this perception leaves a persistent, nagging feeling of insecurity. This perpetual sense of unease can lead to anxiety and depression.

By acknowledging negative perceptions, you can move forward toward a view of life that is neither unrealistically rosy nor unrelentingly gray. Acknowledging your pace, patterns, and perceptions allows you to control them, altering them to support your optimism, hope, and joy, even when life throws you a curve.

Recover Your Joy

It's safe to say that one thing you forgot through your struggle with depression is how to have *fun*. Admit it, some party-pooper part of you just rolled its eyes and mumbled that "fun" is for other people. The best you can hope for, you think, is not to be disappointed.

I know, because that's how I felt after months of having all my senses—including my sense of humor—bleached and hung out to dry by depression. It was as if the candy was stripped out of life and only a dry mouthful of cotton was left. Live like that very long, and the words *pleasure* and *enjoyment* start to sound like a foreign language.

But it's instructive to notice that the word *enjoyment* means "the process of taking pleasure in something." *Process. Taking.* These are active words, things we purposely do and participate in.

135

You can sit and wait for joy to strike spontaneously, and it sometimes does. But why would you want to wait when it's possible to make it happen for yourself today? As with so many other things we've discussed, the power of enjoyment is triggered by choice.

Start by silencing your inner critic, who pronounces judgment on every possible source of fun . . . before you even try it! A rafting excursion? Too wet, too dangerous. A salsa dance class with friends? Too embarrassing. A day at the amusement park? Too childish, too expensive, too loud, too many lines. The good news is, it's possible to displace objections like these with a determined decision to "just do it." Will this test the boundaries of your comfort zone? Of course. That's what makes it fun!

Next, make room for humor and lightheartedness all through your day. Turn off the news and start a romantic comedy movie marathon or binge on old sitcom episodes or performances by stand-up comedians. Spend time around people who make you laugh and push you to lighten up. Make it your mission to laugh and smile so readily that people begin to wonder what you know that they don't.

It's up to you: sit on shore or grab a surfboard and play.

Refuse to Retreat

Your life is a story. Like all stories, yours involves a hero (you), a journey (the battles you've fought), and a prize (lifelong wellness). In fact, that progression is found in every story ever told, from ancient myths sung by firelight, to fairy tales, to modern blockbuster films. Embedded in all stories is a blueprint for human evolution. In other words, struggling is not failure, it's part of being human. It's how we change and grow stronger. As Joseph Campbell, the great mythologist and author of *The Hero with a Thousand Faces*, once wrote, "It is by going down into the abyss that we recover the treasures of life. Where you stumble, there lies your treasure."[2]

That's great news. It means you need not look back on depression with regret, but rather with hope that you've survived the ordeal in order to be stronger and better than ever.

But there is another universal truth about heroes you need to know as you look ahead to the rest of your life. True heroes—the ones we love most when we find them in books and movies and real-life stories—are never content to passively let events happen to them. They are the ones who, when things look darkest and all hope seems lost, refuse to give up or give in. They are tenacious beyond all reason. They stubbornly believe in what others say is impossible. They get back up again and again when knocked down.

Now that you've fought your way to the treasure of wellness on your own journey, it's important to dig in your heels and tap into the heroic determination to never, ever give it back. The future is yours. Defend it. Fight for it like the hero warriors you admire most in your favorite stories.

APPENDIX A

Troubled Teenagers

Why They Are at Risk
and What Can Be Done

In the Netflix teen drama series *13 Reasons Why*, high school student Hannah Baker commits suicide, leaving behind a box of cassette tapes explaining the reasons she killed herself. Clay, a former crush, mysteriously receives copies of tapes—as do Hannah's frenemies incriminated in the recordings. The show's four seasons revolve around the aftermath of Hannah's suicide and her revelations.

The show, wildly popular among teens, created controversy as fans and critics expressed their praise and concerns. Many praised the show for creating a way to have conversations about suicidal thoughts, mental illness, sexual assault, and bullying. Others criticized the implied messages that parents and school counselors aren't viable sources of help or that killing yourself is a good way to draw attention to the message you want to leave behind.

Researchers at the University of Michigan School of Medicine surveyed eighty-seven teens and discovered half had watched at least one episode. Among those, half again reported that watching the show had put them at a higher risk of suicide. The study also revealed that during the show's first season, internet searches for "how to commit suicide" increased by 26 percent.[1]

One thing on which both fans and critics agree is that, for better or worse, the show certainly shined a spotlight on issues surrounding teens and suicide.

Statistics on Teen Suicide

Something else no one can deny is that the suicide rate among our teenagers is climbing.

A trusted colleague of mine, Dr. Michael Gurian, calls the rising suicide rates among young people a growing crisis and warns that teen mental health issues are nothing short of an epidemic. "The mental health of teenagers is becoming increasingly fragile," Dr. Gurian says. "Many of us believe teen mental health issues are becoming epidemic. Wherever we look, we see immense loneliness and confusion in teen communities. From neurotoxins affecting the teen brain to the effects of trauma and social media, we are raising a generation of teens at risk of brain development issues."[2]

Here are some disturbing statistics related to teen suicide:

- Between 2000 and 2007, the suicide rate for persons aged fifteen to nineteen was stable, but it has been climbing since 2007. Between 2007 and 2014, teen suicide increased by 3 percent annually. In 2014, teen suicide began increasing by 10 percent each year.[3]
- Currently in the United States, suicide is the second leading cause of death among young people, exceeded only by automobile accidents.

- According to a CDC 2019 Youth Risk Behavior Survey, approximately one in five teens reported seriously considering suicide and one in six had made a suicide plan.[4]

In chapter 6, we discussed warning signs indicating that someone you love might be at risk of suicide. In addition to the red flags mentioned in that chapter, teenagers can exhibit additional signs, including sexual promiscuity, truancy, behavior problems in school, or falling grades.

Like adults, teenagers can be particularly vulnerable during times of crisis, but sometimes those crises look different than they do for adults. It can be tempting for adults to look at the life of today's teen and think, *They don't have the grown-up pressures I have. They must not be struggling.* But the list of circumstances and events that can make a teenager feel like life is not worth living is a long one. Conflicts with parents, unrequited love, a fight with a best friend, interactions with bullies, the divorce of parents, the addiction or mental illness of a parent, sexual harassment or abuse, gender dysphoria, the suicide of a friend or acquaintance, even the health problems of a sibling can be red-flag circumstances indicating a teen is at greater risk of suicidal ideations.

We make a mistake when we dismiss red-flag signs and circumstances, thinking of these things as "normal teenaged angst."

The truth is that teenagers today are under what is arguably an unprecedented amount of pressure and challenges. One of the reasons is that social media has poured gasoline on centuries-old fodder for normal teen angst like peer pressure, loneliness, insecurities, and bullying. It has also created a bubble of secrecy around sometimes dangerous influences that have 24/7 access to our children. In other words, if your teen has a smartphone, it's possible that you have no idea what pressures and influences they are under.

Of course, it's possible for a parent to understand the many challenges facing today's teens and to feel overwhelmed as a result.

Dr. Gurian writes: "As parents, we adore our children. We will sacrifice anything for them. But we are not sure what they need nor how to help them get assistance, services, or medicine. We are also desperately unsure of what limits to put on their social media use, eating and sleeping habits, and relational dramas."[5]

What Can Parents Do?

Know the warning signs and take them seriously. Don't assume that a teen's depression, anxiety, ADHD, or substance abuse is normal for their age and will resolve itself in time. Obtain help for your teen right away.

If you are overwhelmed and don't know how to address the issues facing your teen, don't give up. Get information. Talk to professionals; even before your teen is ready to accept help, get support and guidance for yourself.

Keep communication lines open with your teen. Ask questions. As I mentioned in an earlier chapter, asking your teen if they are depressed or having thoughts about suicide will not encourage suicidal ideations if they are not having them already. Above all, listen. For people of all ages, feeling unknown and unheard can contribute to hopeless thoughts such as, *No one would miss me if I were gone.* Listening is a gift that tells someone they are valued— and may be an initial step toward inner healing.

Finally, look for ways to work with other parents, educators, and professionals in your community. Suicide prevention programs and training in schools are vastly underfunded and can't meet the need. Meet with teachers, school counselors, and other parents to see how you can help. Talk to local government officials about additional funding and resources as well.

The Science behind Suicide

How Physiology, Brain Chemistry, and Other Factors Contribute to a Drastic Decision

The motive for any serious study of suicide should be obvious—to *prevent* it. It does us no good to understand the broad cultural factors or personal life circumstances known to trigger suicidality if that knowledge leaves us no closer to helping people make a different choice.

But that goal inevitably leads to a good question: Is it possible to prevent suicide by learning to reliably *predict* it? Clearly that's what is behind the lists of risk factors you'll find in guidelines published by every suicide prevention organization in existence—and in this book, for that matter. That approach—as helpful as it is—employs broad strokes that are useful for spotting tendencies but not specific intentions. Some scientists, however, have devoted their careers to answering the question in a much more concrete way. They believe that a person's likelihood of committing suicide may be determined, in part, by tangible physical or chemical imbalances in the brain, or by genetic predilection—and that those conditions may leave detectable traces in the body that can be acted on *before* a suicide attempt.

It's an enticing prospect—and one that has been given new life in recent years by some tantalizing research investigating a number of possible candidate markers. In a moment we'll look more closely at some of those.

A Few Caveats

Let's consider a few big-picture factors at play that form a realistic foundation to the conversation about science and suicide.

1. There is no "off" switch in the brain.

None of the research I've surveyed claims to be on the trail of a magic-bullet solution to the problem of suicide. All of them acknowledge that the tendency to harm oneself is influenced by a complex array of factors and forces, no one of which calls all the shots. An American Academy of Pediatrics report on adolescent suicide acknowledged that while "suicide is the second leading cause of death for adolescents 15 to 19 years old . . . suicide risk can only be reduced, not eliminated, and risk factors provide no more than guidance."[1]

Nevertheless, what drives the research is the prospect of finding new and more predictable factors that rise above mere guidance to give care providers clear signs of elevated risk.

2. Searching for the signal in the noise is tough.

It is widely accepted that a majority of people who take their lives suffer from major depression or some other mental disorder.

In recent years, a lot of study has gone into identifying physical causes and indicators for those as well, with some success. But only a small percentage of depressed people go on to take their lives, leaving researchers with a daunting challenge: how to control for (i.e., factor out) the presence of such overlapping influences and zeroing in on those markers that may point specifically toward increased suicide risk, not just mental health issues in general.

For example, as we'll see shortly, fluctuations in serotonin levels in the brain have been identified in some victims of suicide. Yet serotonin has long been implicated as a possible factor in depression—research that has fueled the development of some popular antidepressant medications. That isn't enough to stop the search for suicide predictors in its tracks, but it does make the task more difficult.

3. Results are confusing at best.

Some studies point to a deficit of certain neurotransmitters in suicide risk, while others see an abundance of the same chemicals as a possible culprit. One prominent researcher—Nadine Melhem, an epidemiologist at the University of Pittsburgh School of Medicine—puts it like this: "It's a confusing literature. . . . Almost every [possible] finding has been reported."[2]

Again, that doesn't invalidate the search. It probably has more to do with variances in study structure, methodology, size, and composition of the population of participants than actual conflicting findings. However, at this stage in the quest we must keep in mind that no clear pathway has yet emerged.

4. Ethics are a limiting factor.

Most researchers are hesitant to enlist people for study who are known to be at extreme risk of suicide already—because of recent attempts or other overt evidence. The fear is that such people may not be able to make an informed decision about voluntary participation, or that study methods may inadvertently make matters worse for them. Not all scientists agree with that cautious approach, however. Writing for the journal *Nature*, Sara Reardon reported:

> Michael Minzenberg, a psychiatrist at the University of California, San Francisco, knows these concerns all too well: he studies suicidal people with schizophrenia. Many of these people struggle with basic life skills, such as keeping a job or finding housing. "They're a challenging group to treat, let alone to study," Minzenberg says.
>
> He and other researchers who study suicidal people say that they treat them with special care—and that the overall benefits of such studies outweigh any risks. "In most clinical trials, people at high risk of suicide are excluded, so we don't know how to treat them," [Fabrice] Jollant [McGill University, Montreal, Canada] says. "We need to assess this population, not just say 'exclude them from trials.'"[3]

5. On a positive note, the research is paying off already—from the patients' point of view.

As I've discussed in previous chapters, a stereotype exists labeling anyone who even seriously contemplates suicide as being "broken" or "weak" or any number of other pejorative descriptors. Learning that scientists believe there may be important physical influences sometimes provides a needed emotional boost to patients. Again, Dr. Nadine Melhem:

> When we introduce biological markers, just like [for] any other area of medicine, then stigma will be reduced at the level of the patient. Patients are often surprised to hear that researchers are studying the biology underlying suicide, because they've been thinking that this is a behavioral flaw in their character, and they feel guilty about it. That's part of the stigma that we want to break.[4]

Professional Motivation

In some respects, this kind of research is as important to doctors and other caregivers as it is to the people struggling with the specter of suicide in their families and communities. A client I worked with early in my career—and before the search for physical factors gained the traction it has today—illustrates why.

As a younger professional, I was a little intimidated when a well-established and respected psychiatrist sought counseling from me. Carol was someone I knew by reputation in my community, and though physicians and other caregivers are not immune to all the emotional and psychological challenges everyone faces, I wondered how I could help a person with so much more experience in the field than me. Her story opened my eyes to just how far and wide the devastating effects of suicide run in our society.

Part of Carol's duty as an on-call psychiatrist at a local hospital was to evaluate people in emergency care after they had experienced extreme mental distress—severe depression, acute anxiety, a psychotic episode, and so on. Her job was to decide which of them needed to remain under observation—in particular those who might present a suicide risk—and which should be released.

"I was well trained in what to look for," she told me. "Sure, we were dealing with the human mind, which is always an imprecise practice, but I was confident that our methods were sound and effective."

Until she met Franklin. At thirty-seven, he had struggled with depression and anxiety for years—a condition that grew so severe he was forced to leave his career as a paramedic. He went back to college and became an elementary school teacher instead. On the night he was brought to the emergency room, Franklin had been found in the street outside a restaurant where he had just had dinner alone. He sat on the center line cross-legged, staring into space, unresponsive.

"During my evaluation, Franklin told me he'd 'blacked out' as he left the restaurant and had no idea how he came to be in the road," Carol said. "He seemed as alarmed by the incident as those who had found him and hurriedly dialed 9-1-1. He had been taking antidepressant medication for several years, and reported no problems with the dosage."

Franklin talked fondly about his students and how he hoped they would not learn of this incident. Based on Franklin's history and his cooperative state of mind in the hospital, Carol judged that Franklin should be released. She set up a follow-up appointment in a few days and saw him to the door.

That night Franklin took an entire bottle of prescription pain medication and died. The news hit Carol hard.

"My first thought was of the children in his class and to wonder how on earth he could subject them to the trauma of losing their teacher to suicide," she told me in anguish. "Most of all, though, I can't stop thinking about what I missed. Was there an obvious clue that I was too distracted or too busy to notice? How many others have I released who went on to harm themselves and I don't even know it?"

Carol was traumatized by the very question we asked at the beginning of this book: *Why?* But for caregivers the question goes deeper and becomes, *Is there a concrete way to take the guesswork out of evaluation?* Medical journalist Catherine Offord, writing in *The Scientist*, says:

> It's still a dilemma facing anyone attempting to provide care for people at risk of suicide. Today's clinicians often rely on patients to report their intentions in order to decide on appropriate interventions. But the approach has limitations. One 2019 meta-analysis of studies on suicidal ideation found that around 60 percent of people who ended their lives had denied having suicidal thoughts when asked by a clinician or doctor in the weeks or months before their death.[5]

Here's the point: While the quest for identifiable and reliable physical markers pointing to elevated risk of suicide is still in its infancy, the deep desire to find and understand them is shared by many who've been affected by this tragedy.

Bread Crumbs in the Forest

Without getting too technical, here is a brief survey of current areas of research.

Neurochemicals. The brain has multiple ways to respond to stress, but the one most thoroughly investigated with respect to suicide is the production of the hormone cortisol. It has many functions in the body, one of them being stress regulation. Serotonin—sometimes known as the "happy chemical" for its role in mood regulation—has also been a focus of recent research. Increasingly, scientists are interested in how these two form a complex system and work together—or don't, in the case of certain mental disorders, including suicide. Much of the literature focuses on what's known as the "hypothalamic-pituitary-adrenal (HPA) axis" and what clues the relative abundance and function of these chemicals might hold.

Another neurochemical under scrutiny is gamma-aminobutyric acid (commonly known as GABA), an abundant neural activity inhibitor in the brain. Michael Poulter, a neuroscientist at the Robarts Research Institute at the University of Western Ontario, describes it like this: "If you think about the gas pedal and brakes on a car, GABA is the brakes."[6]

Studies have shown that depressed people who committed suicide had an abnormal distribution of receptors for the chemical, inhibiting proper function. Ultimately, these findings reveal that suicidal brains differ from other brains in multiple ways—in other words, "We're really dealing with some sort of biological imbalance," Poulter says. "It's not an attitude problem."[7]

Neuroinflammation. A number of clues point to the possibility that inflammation of the brain—and the body's response to it—may lead to a higher risk of suicide. One study in Denmark examined health records of seven million patients over three decades who had been hospitalized for infectious disease and calculated a "40 percent greater probability of suicide" among them.[8]

149

Researchers acknowledge other factors could be in play as well, such as the effect of medications used to treat the diseases. However, that's not the first time inflammation of the brain and mental health have been linked. *The Scientist* reports:

> Elevated suicide risk has previously been reported in people with autoimmune disorders and traumatic brain injury—conditions that, like infections, typically involve inflammation. . . . While depression is not thought of as an inflammatory disease, signs of neuroinflammation in the brain have been repeatedly documented in people who suffer from depression, and a number of anti-inflammatory drugs show antidepressant effects.[9]

This may eventually make it possible to predict suicide risk by detecting signs of associated inflammation.

Neuroimaging. Scientists are increasingly using positron emission tomography (PET) and magnetic resonance imaging (MRI) technology to take snapshots of what's going on in the brain. For example, a 2017 study by University of Pittsburgh psychiatry professor David Brent and colleagues used functional MRI to image the brains of thirty-four people as they contemplated words such as *death*, *trouble*, and *carefree*. An assessment of the study said:

> Using machine learning algorithms to process the data, the team could distinguish between people who were thinking about suicide, as self-reported during the study, and those who weren't with 91 percent accuracy. Among those who were, the team identified people who'd already attempted suicide with 94 percent accuracy.[10]

Genetics and Epigenetics. It has long been recognized that a family history of suicide statistically raises a person's risk of suicidal behavior in life, though the magnitude of the identified risk varies between studies. Some of the other research cited above may offer a partial explanation for the observed link. If certain physical traits contribute to suicide risk, then it might stand to reason that those are passed from generation to generation within a family.

The field of *epigenetics* may offer a link between more traditional risk factors and physical markers. This is the study of how any organism responds to environmental stress through changes in how its genes are *expressed*, without altering the actual DNA sequence. Simply, researchers are finding that people who suffered trauma early in life—such as physical or sexual abuse—often exhibit detectable changes in how certain genetically driven body functions operate. These might even include cortisol and serotonin levels. Another example takes us back to the discussion of GABA. Medical journalist Melinda Wenner, reporting in *Scientific American*, says:

> Interestingly, this GABA receptor problem is not the result of abnormal or mutated genes. Rather the change is epigenetic, meaning some environmental influence affected how often the relevant genes were expressed—that is, made into proteins.[11]

Researchers point out that not all victims of childhood abuse go on to commit suicide. It may be that analyzing epigenetic changes could identify those at greater risk.

The Whole Body

If nothing else, this discussion serves to illustrate the importance of the whole-person approach I emphasize in all my work. Treating suicide as simply an "attitude problem," as one researcher put it, is as shortsighted as expecting science to develop a pill to solve the problem in one stroke. To fully address this tragic issue, we must follow every lead—and then never lose sight of how they all work together.

Finally, let's not forget that the human body is not simply a machine but a dynamic creation and expression of God's love and creative power. What has gone wrong can be put right through reason and dogged effort, but also through faith in the Great Healer.

"I will say of the LORD, 'He is my refuge and my fortress, my God, in whom I trust'" (Ps. 91:2).

APPENDIX C

Reasons to Hope on the Road Ahead

Innovative Strategies in the Battle against Suicide

When it comes to suicide, a hallmark characteristic is hopelessness. And yet in the battle against suicide, there is every reason for great hope. Innovative strategies continue to be implemented, with more on the horizon.

Some of these strategies focus on identifying people at higher risk, while others focus on innovative interventions and treatments. Here are seven promising strategies that are currently in use or on the horizon:

1. New protocols for universal screening in health care facilities. Since 2007, the Joint Commission—the standards-setting body that issues accreditations and certifications for twenty-two thousand health care organizations and programs—has required suicide risk screening for patients being admitted to psychiatric hospitals or units. A growing number of emergency rooms are also implementing screening for suicide risk.

The need for health care professionals in every specialty to know how to assess and manage suicide risk makes sense. Research shows that, in the months before their death, between 40 and 75 percent of people who commit suicide have been in contact with primary care doctors for issues not related to mental health. One study of elderly people who committed suicide determined that three out of four had seen their primary care doctor in the month before their death.

This means that health care professionals, despite not being in the mental health field, may be in a position to identify people at risk—given the right tools and protocols.

2. Training non–health care professionals to recognize warning signs. In Hong Kong, debt counselors for gambling addicts are receiving training to help them recognize signs of suicidal ideations in their clients.[1] And an increasing number of schools are offering suicide prevention training to all teachers and staff members—not just school counselors. After all, knowing how to spot when someone is signaling their distress—and more importantly, knowing how to respond—doesn't need to be solely the responsibility of mental health providers. The more our society is equipped to help, the better.

The American Association of Suicidology has developed an acronym representing some of the most common warning signs. Using the acronym "IS PATH WARM?" can help you remember some of the signs that someone may be heading toward danger:

Ideation (suicidal thoughts)
Substance abuse

Purposelessness

Anxiety

Trapped

Hopelessness/helplessness

Withdrawal

Anger

Recklessness

Mood changes

3. Brain scans are providing a window into the brain and mind.
Researchers are using scanning technology to document differences in the brains of people at greater risk of suicide. Among these are people who have been diagnosed with depression, bipolar disorder, or PTSD.

In one study, after evaluating the differences in brain activity of people with and without suicidal thoughts, researchers were able to create an algorithm that could predict, with a high degree of accuracy, who was in the group of people who had experienced suicidal thoughts and attempts.[2]

Marcel Just, a Carnegie Mellon University professor and co-leader of the study, explained that the study provided a "window into the brain and mind, shedding light on how suicidal individuals think" and might one day be used to determine whether someone is considering suicide.[3]

Other studies have discovered measurable differences in how the brains of at-risk people create and process a neurotransmitter called glutamate. For example, a study led by Dr. Irina Esterlis at Yale University discovered 30 percent more glutamate receptors in the brains of people with PTSD who had considered suicide.[4] And researchers at the University of Illinois at Chicago discovered an overabundance of glutamate in the brain tissue of women who struggled with depression, many of whom had committed suicide.[5]

The most common amino acid in your body, glutamate is found in 90 percent of brain synapses and is essential for learning and memory. But maintaining the right balance of glutamate in the brain is a precision process. Too little glutamate has been linked with insomnia and psychoses. Too much contributes to depression and anxiety, which is why research on this neurotransmitter is so promising for people at risk of suicide.

Brain studies like these and others are creating a growing body of data that is already proving invaluable in the fight against suicide.

4. Positive messaging with a theatrical twist. There can be a stigma associated with asking for help, but positive messages can begin to erase that stigma. One example is a street theater group in India that has embraced an innovative way to get that message into the public.

The Indian theater group Nalanthana wrote and performed a series of plays in which suicidal characters reconsidered their plans when friends intervened with information about a local mental health agency.[6] In addition to teaching that suicidal thoughts are not a one-way street to suicide—that there is help and hope—the street plays provide encouragement to speak up and intervene when someone you know exhibits suicidal warning signs.

Similar endeavors are appearing in other parts of the world, including the United States. A program in Montana, for example, uses peer-to-peer, community-based dramatizations to engage and educate audiences. The *Let's Talk* productions feature young adults who create and perform plays that bring awareness and foster conversation about suicide. Performances are followed by actor-audience discussions facilitated by a licensed mental health counselor.[7]

Such programs—utilized increasingly in high schools, colleges, and community groups—are another way to highlight risk factors and potential solutions to the daunting problem of suicide.

5. Predicting suicide risk using electronic health records. Can electronic health records be analyzed to help predict suicide risk? Researchers think so. In fact, one study used 313 demographic and clinical characteristics to assign patients a suicide risk score. The risk scores did prove predictive of future behavior: people with risk scores in the top 5 percent accounted for nearly half of subsequent suicides and suicide attempts.[8]

The accuracy of the predictive scores was impressive—up to 94 percent—meaning that this tool, once perfected and implemented, may provide an effective way to identify people at greater risk of suicide.

6. Using food to lift our mood. Science is still working to understand the connection between the gut and the brain, but the connection is so great that the gastrointestinal tract is often called the "second brain."

What does this have to do with feelings such as depression and anxiety that can make someone more prone to suicide? For starters, the gastrointestinal tract produces about 95 percent of the serotonin that regulates sleep, appetite, moods, and even pain. So it stands to reason that when our intestinal tract isn't happy, *we* aren't happy.

Nutritional psychiatry is the growing practice of using food choices to improve mental health. Particularly when it comes to depression and anxiety—two major contributors to suicide risk— what we eat really does matter.

For example, in one study, researchers identified twelve nutrients that have antidepressant properties: folate, iron, long-chain omega-3 fatty acids, magnesium, potassium, selenium, thiamine, zinc, and vitamins A, B6, B12, and C.[9]

In another study, microbiologist Jeroen Raes studied the gut bacteria of more than one thousand participants and discovered that subjects who had been diagnosed with depression were lacking two kinds of healthy microbes, while hosting a greater number of bacteria associated with inflammation.[10]

We are still learning about the link between gut and mental health, but the connection appears to promise hope and help for all of us.

7. Collaborative care. This strategy brings a team approach to the initial level of primary care. When a primary care physician collaborates with behavioral care specialists such as counselors or social workers and mental health experts such as psychiatrists, the patient is the clear winner.

Dr. Anna Ratzliff, a national expert on collaborative care, is a professor at the University of Washington's Department of Psychiatry and Behavioral Sciences and the codirector of the AIMS Center (Advancing Integrated Mental Health Solutions). During a 2018 National Institute of Mental Health presentation,[11] she described a study where 1,801 patients were divided into two groups. The first group received typical care from their primary care physician. The second group was assigned to a collaborative team.

Among those receiving collaborative health care, twice as many people reported improvements in depressive symptoms than those receiving traditional care from their primary physician. Collaborative care patients also reported less physical pain.

Dr. Ratzliff added, "The purpose of really delivering collaborative care is to get patients back living their lives. And that's important when you think about suicide prevention, right? Because when people are depressed, they become hopeless and that puts them at greatest risk for wanting to act on suicide ideation."[12]

Acknowledgments

My sincere gratitude for making this book happen goes to . . .

Keith Wall, who has teamed with me to get these lifesaving words of hope on the page.

Alex Field, founder and agent at The Bindery literary agency, and his associate Ingrid Beck, who are highly skilled professionals and passionate about books that change lives.

Vicki Crumpton, executive editor at Revell, whose top-notch expertise and consistent encouragement helped this book reach its full potential.

The entire Revell team—designers, copyeditors, marketing specialists, and others—who are true partners and valuable contributors to this important book.

Notes

Prologue: Hope amid Heartache

1. Mental Health America, "The State of Mental Health in America," https://mhanational.org/issues/state-mental-health-america.

2. Peggy Christidis, Luona Lin, and Karen Stamm, "An Unmet Need for Mental Health Services," *Monitor on Psychology* 49, no. 4 (April 2018), https://www.apa.org/monitor/2018/04/datapoint.

3. World Health Organization, "Mental Health and Substance Abuse," https://www.who.int/mental_health/prevention/suicide/suicideprevent/en.

Chapter 1: Lifelines

1. To delve much deeper into this topic, see the book I coauthored with my colleague Dr. Tim Clinton, *Am I Codependent? Key Questions to Ask about Your Relationships* (Grand Rapids: Revell, 2019).

2. Mayo Clinic, "Caregiver Stress: Tips for Taking Care of Yourself," last updated December 16, 2020, https://www.mayoclinic.org/healthy-lifestyle/stress-management/in-depth/caregiver-stress/art-20044784.

3. Jeffrey Foote, Carrie Wilkens, Nicole Kosanke, and Stephanie Higgs, *Beyond Addiction: How Science and Kindness Help People Change* (New York: Scribner, 2014), 102.

Chapter 2: Why Here, Why Now?

1. These statistics are from the CDC, "Preventing Suicide Factsheet 2021," https://www.cdc.gov/suicide/pdf/preventing-suicide-factsheet-2021-508.pdf; "Suicide Rising across the US," last updated June 7, 2018, https://www.cdc.gov/vitalsigns/suicide/index.html.

2. Katherine Schaeffer, "6 Facts about Economic Inequality in the U.S.," FactTank, February 7, 2020, https://www.pewresearch.org/fact-tank/2020/02/07/6-facts-about-economic-inequality-in-the-u-s.

3. Bill Fay, "Demographics of Debt," Debt.org, last updated May 19, 2020, https://www.debt.org/faqs/americans-in-debt/demographics.

4. Marie K. Shanahan, "How News Sites' Online Comments Helped Build Our Hateful Electorate," *The Conversation*, December 14, 2016, https://theconversa tion.com/how-news-sites-online-comments-helped-build-our-hateful-electorate -70170.

5. Gregory Jantz, *Social Media and Depression: How to Be Healthy and Happy in the Digital Age* (Peabody, MA: Rose Publishing, forthcoming).

6. Centers for Disease Control, "Selected Health Conditions and Risk Factors, by Age: United States, Selected Years 1988–1994 through 2015–2016," 2018, https://www.cdc.gov/nchs/data/hus/2018/021.pdf.

7. National Institute of Diabetes and Digestive and Kidney Diseases, "Health Risks of Being Overweight," February 2015, https://www.niddk.nih.gov/health -information/weight-management/health-risks-overweight.

8. Jeffrey M. Jones, "U.S. Church Membership Down Sharply in Past Two Decades," Gallup, April 18, 2019, https://news.gallup.com/poll/248837/church -membership-down-sharply-past-two-decades.aspx.

9. Mel Walker, "Why Is Church Membership in a Decline?," Christianity .com, April 1, 2020, https://www.christianity.com/wiki/church/why-is-church -membership-in-a-decline.html.

Chapter 3: Why They Do It

1. Centers for Disease Control and Prevention, "Suicide Rising across the US," last updated June 7, 2018, https://www.cdc.gov/vitalsigns/suicide/infographic .html#graphic3.

2. Louise Bradvik, "Suicide Risk and Mental Disorders," *International Journal of Environmental Research and Public Health*, September 17, 2018, https://www .ncbi.nlm.nih.gov/pmc/articles/PMC6165520.

3. Gregory Jantz, *Healing Depression for Life* (Carol Stream, IL: Tyndale, 2019), 2.

4. These comments appeared in "Psychosis Predicts Suicide Thoughts, Plans, Attempts," Healio, August 30, 2017, https://www.healio.com/news/psychiatry /20170830/psychosis-predicts-suicide-thoughts-plans-attempts. The study cited is Evelyn J. Bromet et al., "Association between Psychotic Experiences and Subsequent Suicidal Thoughts and Behaviors," *JAMA Psychiatry* 74, no. 11 (2017): 1136–44, and can be accessed at https://jamanetwork.com/journals/jamapsychiatry /fullarticle/2652448.

5. "Psychosis Predicts Suicide Thoughts, Plans, Attempts."

6. Substance Abuse and Mental Health Services Administration (SAMHSA), "Substance Use and Suicide: A Nexus Requiring a Public Health Approach," In Brief, 2016, https://store.samhsa.gov/sites/default/files/d7/priv/sma16-4935.pdf.

7. Matthew Tull, "The Connection between PTSD and Suicide," Verywell Mind, updated March 22, 2020, https://www.verywellmind.com/ptsd-and-suicide-2797540.

8. Elsevier, "Burden of Physical Health Conditions Linked to Increased Risk of Suicide," *ScienceDaily*, June 12, 2017, https://www.sciencedaily.com/releases /2017/06/170612094032.htm.

9. David Owens, Judith Horrocks, and Allan House, "Fatal and Non-Fatal Repetition of Self-Harm," *British Journal of Psychiatry* (January 2, 2018): 193–99; quoted in Mental Health America, "Suicide," https://www.mhanational.org/conditions/suicide.

Chapter 4: Who Is at High Risk?

1. MedicineNet, "Suicide," last updated April 1, 2011, https://www.medicine net.com/script/main/art.asp?articlekey=84760.

2. American Foundation for Suicide Prevention, "Suicide Facts and Figures: United States 2020," https://www.datocms-assets.com/12810/1587128056-usfacts figuresflyer-2.pdf.

3. American Foundation for Suicide Prevention, "Suicide Statistics," March 1, 2020, https://afsp.org/suicide-statistics.

4. National Center for Biotechnology Information (NCBI), "Appendix D: Groups with Increased Suicide Risk," *2012 National Strategy for Suicide Prevention*, https://www.ncbi.nlm.nih.gov/books/NBK109909.

5. Stephen Rodrick, "All-American Despair," *Rolling Stone*, May 30, 2019, https://www.rollingstone.com/culture/culture-features/suicide-rate-america -white-men-841576.

6. NCBI, "Appendix D."

7. Mannat Mohanjeet Singh, Shradha S. Parsekar, and Sreekumaran N. Nair, "An Epidemiological Overview of Child Sexual Abuse," *Journal of Family Medicine and Primary Care* 3, no. 4 (2014): 430–35, https://www.ncbi.nlm.nih.gov /pmc/articles/PMC4311357.

8. Singh et al., "Epidemiological Overview."

9. Leo Shane III, "New Veteran Suicide Numbers Raise Concerns among Experts Hoping for Positive News," *Military Times*, October 9, 2019, https://www .militarytimes.com/news/pentagon-congress/2019/10/09/new-veteran-suicide -numbers-raise-concerns-among-experts-hoping-for-positive-news.

10. VA Office of Mental Health and Suicide Prevention, *VA National Suicide Data Report 2005–2016*, September 2018, https://www.mentalhealth.va.gov/docs /data-sheets/OMHSP_National_Suicide_Data_Report_2005-2016_508.pdf.

11. Shane, "New Veteran Suicide Numbers."

12. MedicineNet, "Suicide."

13. Cora Peterson et al., "Suicide Rates by Industry and Occupation—National Violent Death Reporting System, 32 States, 2016," *Morbidity and Mortality Weekly Report*, January 24, 2020, https://www.cdc.gov/mmwr/volumes/69/wr /mm6903a1.htm.

14. Brittany Lahoda, "Mental Illness and Suicide in Dental School: Fighting the Stigma," ADA Center for Professional Success, https://success.ada.org/en/wellness /mental-illness-and-suicide-in-dental-school.

15. Peterson et al., "Suicide Rates by Industry and Occupation."

Chapter 5: Setting the Record Straight

1. National Alliance on Mental Illness, "Risk of Suicide," August 2019, https:// www.nami.org/About-Mental-Illness/Common-with-Mental-Illness/Risk-of -Suicide.

2. University of California, Los Angeles, "Putting Feelings into Words Produces Therapeutic Effects in the Brain," *ScienceDaily*, June 22, 2007, https://www.science daily.com/releases/2007/06/070622090727.htm.

3. Michael Esang and Saeed Ahmed, "A Closer Look at Substance Use and Suicide," *American Journal of Psychiatry Residents' Journal* (June 2018): 6, https:// psychiatryonline.org/doi/full/10.1176/appi.ajp-rj.2018.130603.

Chapter 6: Signs and Symptoms

1. Centers for Disease Control and Prevention, "#BeThere to Help Prevent Suicide," last updated December 16, 2020, https://www.cdc.gov/injury/features /be-there-prevent-suicide/index.html.

2. J. Michael Bostwick et al., "Suicide Attempt as a Risk Factor for Completed Suicide: Even More Lethal Than We Knew," *American Journal of Psychiatry* 173, no. 11 (November 1, 2016): 1094–1100, https://www.ncbi.nlm.nih.gov/pmc/articles /PMC5510596.

3. Mark A. Reger, Ian H. Stanley, and Thomas E. Joiner, "Suicide Mortality and Coronavirus Disease 2019—A Perfect Storm?," *JAMA Psychiatry* 77, no. 11 (2020): 1093–94, https://jamanetwork.com/journals/jamapsychiatry/fullarticle /2764584?guestAccessKey=c40eefb2-c634-47ed-b3c3-f00b005e3cf2&utm_.

4. W. Vaughn McCall, "The Correlation between Sleep Disturbance and Suicide," *Psychiatric Times* 32, no. 9 (September 30, 2015), https://www.psychiatric times.com/view/correlation-between-sleep-disturbance-and-suicide.

5. McCall, "Correlation between Sleep Disturbance and Suicide."

Chapter 7: Descent into Darkness

1. Manfred F. R. Kets de Vries, "Dealing with Disappointment," *Harvard Business Review*, August 22, 2018, https://hbr.org/2018/08/dealing-with-disappoint ment.

2. De Vries, "Dealing with Disappointment."

3. William Ward, *Today in the Word* (April 1989), quoted in Grace Quotes, https://gracequotes.org/author-quote/william-ward.

4. Wendy Wisner, "11 Quotes about Depression That Will Make You Feel Less Alone," *The Talkspace Voice* (blog), May 29, 2020, https://www.talkspace.com /blog/depression-quotes-loneliness-lonely.

5. Mayo Clinic Staff, "Depression (Major Depressive Disorder)," February 3, 2018, https://www.mayoclinic.org/diseases-conditions/depression.

6. Mayo Clinic Staff, "Depression."

Chapter 8: Step In and Speak Up

1. "How and Why the 5 Steps Can Help," National Suicide Prevention Lifeline #BeThe1To, https://www.bethe1to.com/bethe1to-steps-evidence.

2. T. Dazzi et al., "Does Asking about Suicide and Related Behaviours Induce Suicidal Ideation? What Is the Evidence?," *Psychological Medicine* 44, no. 16 (December 2014): 3361–33, https://pubmed.ncbi.nlm.nih.gov/24998511.

3. "Duration of Suicidal Crises," Harvard T. H. Chan School of Public Health, https://www.hsph.harvard.edu/means-matter/means-matter/duration.

4. E. David Klonsky and Alexis M. May, "The Three-Step Theory (3ST): A New Theory of Suicide Rooted in the 'Ideation-to-Action' Framework," *International Journal of Cognitive Therapy* 8, no. 2 (June 2015), https://guilfordjournals.com/doi/abs/10.1521/ijct.2015.8.2.114?journalCode=ijct.

5. Harvard School of Public Health, "Duration of Suicidal Crises."

6. Madelyn S. Gould et al., "Impact of Applied Suicide Intervention Skills Training on the National Suicide Prevention Lifeline," *Suicide and Life-Threatening Behavior* 43, no. 6 (December 2013): 676–91, https://pubmed.ncbi.nlm.nih.gov/23889494.

7. "Follow-Up Care Supports the Transition of Individuals Who Are in Suicidal Crisis as They Continue Their Journey towards Recovery," National Suicide Prevention Hotline Follow-Up Matters, https://followupmatters.suicideprevent ionlifeline.org/follow-up-starts-here.

Chapter 9: Whole-Person Wellness

1. Anthony Coniaris, "Healing of Soul and Body," Saint George Greek Orthodox Church, accessed October 3, 2020, http://stgeorgegoc.org/pastors-corner /fr-ricks-sermons/healing-of-soul-and-body.

Chapter 10: Learning to Live Again

1. Amy Novotney, "The Risks of Social Isolation," *Monitor on Psychology* 50, no. 5 (May 2019): 32, https://www.apa.org/monitor/2019/05/ce-corner-isolation.

2. Joseph Campbell, *A Joseph Campbell Companion*, ed. Diane Osbon (New York: Harper Perennial, 1995), 24.

Appendix A: Troubled Teenagers

1. Victor Hong et al., "*13 Reasons Why*: Viewing Patterns and Perceived Impact among Youths at Risk of Suicide," *Psychiatric Services* 70, no. 2 (February 1, 2019): 107–14, https://ps.psychiatryonline.org/doi/10.1176/appi.ps.201800384.

2. Michael Gurian, "Stand Up, Speak Up, To Save Lives," *The Gurian Institute* (blog), November 13, 2017, https://gurianinstitute.com/stand-up-speak-up -to-save-lives/.

3. Sally C. Curtin and Melonie Heron, "Death Rates Due to Suicide and Homicide among Persons Aged 10–24: United States, 2000–2017," *NCHS Data Brief* 352 (October 2019), https://www.cdc.gov/nchs/data/databriefs/db352 -h.pdf.

4. Asha Z. Ivey-Stephenson et al., "Suicidal Ideation and Behaviors among High School Students—Youth Risk Behavior Survey, United States, 2019," Centers for Disease Control and Prevention, August 21, 2020, https://www.cdc.gov/mmwr /volumes/69/su/su6901a6.htm?s_cid=su6901a6_w.

5. Gurian Institute, "Is Children's Mental Health a School Issue or a Parent Issue?," September 26, 2017, https://gurianinstitute.com/is-childrens-mental -health-a-school-issue-or-a-parent-issue.

Appendix B: The Science behind Suicide

1. Benjamin Shain and Committee on Adolescence, "Suicide and Suicide Attempts in Adolescents," *Pediatrics*, June 2016, https://pediatrics.aappublications .org/content/early/2016/06/24/peds.2016-1420.

2. Catherine Offord, "What Neurobiology Can Tell Us about Suicide," *The Scientist*, January 13, 2020, https://www.the-scientist.com/features/what-neuro biology-can-tell-us-about-suicide-66922.

3. Sara Reardon, "Brain Study Seeks Roots of Suicide," *Nature*, November 25, 2015, https://www.nature.com/news/brain-study-seeks-roots-of-suicide-1.18870.

4. Offord, "What Neurobiology Can Tell Us."

5. Offord, "What Neurobiology Can Tell Us."

6. Melinda Wenner, "The Origins of Suicidal Brains," *Scientific American*, February 1, 2009, https://www.scientificamerican.com/article/the-origins-of-suicidal -brains.

7. Wenner, "Origins of Suicidal Brains."

8. Offord, "What Neurobiology Can Tell Us."

9. Offord, "What Neurobiology Can Tell Us."

10. Offord, "What Neurobiology Can Tell Us."

11. Wenner, "Origins of Suicidal Brains."

Appendix C: Reasons to Hope on the Road Ahead

1. Paul Yip et al., "Innovative Approaches in Asia to Identifying Those at Risk for Suicide," in *Suicide and Suicide Prevention in Asia*, ed. Herbert Hendin et al. (Geneva, Switzerland: World Health Organization, 2018), chapter 6, https://apps .who.int/iris/bitstream/handle/10665/43929/9789241596893_eng.pdf.

2. Angela Chen, "Algorithm Can Identify Suicidal People Using Brain Scans," *The Verge*, October 30, 2017, https://www.theverge.com/2017/10/30/16570148/neuro science-suicide-mental-health-brain-imagining-fmri-machine-learning-algorithm.

3. Robert Preidt, "Can Brain Scans Predict Suicidal Tendencies?," CBS News, November 1, 2017, https://www.cbsnews.com/news/can-brain-scans-predict-suicidal -tendencies.

4. Emily Underwood, "Brain Scans Could Help Personalize Treatment for People Who Are Depressed or Suicidal," *Science*, August 20, 2019, https://www .sciencemag.org/news/2019/08/brain-scans-could-help-personalize-treatment -people-who-are-depressed-or-suicidal.

5. University of Illinois at Chicago, "Depressed Females Have Over-Active Glutamate Receptor Gene," ScienceDaily, July 30, 2015, https://www.sciencedaily .com/releases/2015/07/150730172348.htm.

6. Yip et al., "Innovative Approaches."

7. Sarah Keller et al., "A Theater Intervention to Promote Communication and Disclosure of Suicidal Ideation," *Journal of Applied Communication Research* 45, no. 3 (2017): 294–312.

8. Gregory E. Simon et al., "Predicting Suicide Attempts and Suicide Deaths Following Outpatient Visits Using Electronic Health Records," *American Journal of Psychiatry* 175, no. 10 (October 1, 2018): 951–60, https://pubmed.ncbi.nlm .nih.gov/29792051.

9. Laura R. LaChance and Drew Ramsey, "Antidepressant Foods: An Evidence-Based Nutrient Profiling System for Depression," *World Journal of Psychiatry* 8, no. 3 (September 20, 2018): 97–104, https://www.ncbi.nlm.nih.gov/pmc/articles/PMC6147775.

10. Elizabeth Pennisi, "Evidence Mounts That Gut Bacteria Can Influence Mood, Prevent Depression," *Science*, February 4, 2019, https://www.sciencemag.org/news/2019/02/evidence-mounts-gut-bacteria-can-influence-mood-prevent-depression.

11. Anna Ratzliff, "Suicide Prevention and the Collaborative Care Model," National Institute of Mental Health webinar, August 23, 2018, https://www.nimh.nih.gov/news/media/2018/suicide-prevention-and-the-collaborative-care-model.shtml.

12. Ratzliff, "Suicide Prevention and the Collaborative Care Model."

Recommended Resources

Suicide Hotlines and Websites

National Suicide Prevention Lifeline: 1-800-273-8255 (TALK).

National Suicide Prevention Lifeline's website: www.suicideprevention lifeline.org.

Substance Abuse and Mental Health Services Association (SAMHSA) National Helpline: 1-800-662-4357

YouthLine: Text teen2teen to 839863, or call 1-877-968-8491.

Organizations Offering Help for Mental Health Issues

American Association of Christian Counselors. www.aacc.net; 1-800-526-8673. This organization equips clinical, pastoral, and lay caregivers with biblical truth and psychosocial insights to assist them as they minister to hurting persons and help them move to personal wholeness. The AACC offers a referral service for local counselors, coaches, and clinics.

American Psychological Association. www.apa.org. The largest association of psychologists in the world, the APA offers access to the latest information on depression and related conditions like ADHD, eating disorders, and suicide.

Anxiety and Depression Association of America. www.adaa.org. This organization provides detailed facts about various conditions including depression and its symptoms.

Brain and Behavior Research Foundation. www.bbrfoundation.org. This site provides information about depression, anxiety, and other related conditions. The foundation provides support for research into depression and related conditions.

Depression and Bipolar Support Alliance. www.dbsalliance.org. This is a self-help organization for patients and family members, providing significant information on depression as well as anxiety and bipolar disorder.

Mental Health America. www.mhanational.org. This is one of the foremost nonprofit organizations in the mental health field providing up-to-date news and information.

National Alliance on Mental Illness. www.nami.org. This organization provides education and support pertaining to a wide variety of mental health conditions.

National Institute of Mental Health. www.nimh.nih.gov. As the country's largest organization focusing on mental health conditions, NIMH publishes detailed information on the latest findings related to depression, anxiety, ADHD, OCD, and related conditions.

Books on Suicide

Blauner, Susan Rose. *How I Stayed Alive When My Brain Was Trying to Kill Me: One Person's Guide to Suicide Prevention.* New York: William Morrow, 2002.

Fine, Carla. *No Time to Say Goodbye: Surviving the Suicide of a Loved One.* New York: Harmony Books, 1999.

Goldsmith, Connie. *Understanding Suicide: A National Epidemic.* Minneapolis: Twenty-First Century Books, 2016.

Jamison, Kay Redfield. *Night Falls Fast: Understanding Suicide.* New York: Vintage, 2000.

Jobes, David. *Managing Suicidal Risk: A Collaborative Approach.* New York: Guilford Press, 2016.

Joiner, Thomas. *Why People Die by Suicide.* Cambridge, MA: Harvard University Press, 2005.

Books on Emotional Health and Depression

Hyman, Mark. *The UltraMind Solution: The Simple Way to Defeat Depression, Overcome Anxiety, and Sharpen Your Mind*. New York: Scribner, 2009.

Jantz, Gregory. *Happy for the Rest of Your Life: Four Steps to Contentment, Hope, and Joy*. Lake Mary, FL: Siloam, 2009.

———. *Healing Depression for Life: The Personalized Approach that Offers New Hope for Lasting Relief*. Carol Stream, IL: Tyndale, 2019.

———. *Healing the Scars of Addiction: Reclaiming Your Life and Moving into a Healthy Future*. Grand Rapids: Revell, 2018.

———. *Healing the Scars of Childhood Abuse: Moving beyond the Past into a Healthy Future*. Grand Rapids: Revell, 2017.

———. *Overcoming Anxiety, Worry, and Fear: Practical Ways to Find Peace*. Grand Rapids: Revell, 2011.

Jantz, Gregory, and Tim Clinton. *Don't Call It Love: Breaking the Cycle of Relationship Dependency*. Grand Rapids: Revell, 2015.

Jones, Keith, ed. *Depression Sourcebook: Health Reference Series*. 4th ed. Detroit: Omnigraphics, 2017.

Korb, Alex. *The Upward Spiral: Using Neuroscience to Reverse the Course of Depression, One Small Change at a Time*. Oakland: New Harbinger Publications, 2015.

Rossman, Martin. *The Worry Solution: Using Your Healing Mind to Turn Stress and Anxiety into Better Health and Happiness*. New York: Harmony, 2010.

Gregory L. Jantz, PhD, is a popular speaker and award-winning author of many books, including *Healing the Scars of Emotional Abuse*, *Healing the Scars of Childhood Abuse*, and *Overcoming Anxiety, Worry, and Fear*. He is the founder of The Center: A Place of Hope, which was voted among the top ten clinics in the nation for healing depression. For more information about Dr. Jantz and The Center, contact:

www.drgregoryjantz.com
www.aplaceofhope.com

Keith Wall, a twenty-five-year publishing veteran, is an award-winning author, magazine editor, radio scriptwriter, and online columnist. He currently writes full time in collaboration with numerous bestselling authors. Keith lives in a mountaintop cabin near Manitou Springs, Colorado.

HOPE AND HEALING
FOR THE VICTIMS
OF EMOTIONAL ABUSE

GREGORY L. JANTZ, PhD
WITH ANN McMURRAY

Healing
the Scars of
Emotional
Abuse

REVISED AND UPDATED

Revell
a division of Baker Publishing Group
www.RevellBooks.com

Available wherever books and ebooks are sold.

It Is Possible to Become Whole and Happy

In this compassionate book, Dr. Gregory Jantz helps you understand the effects of childhood abuse on your emotional, intellectual, physical, relational, and spiritual health. He then walks you through the steps to lasting healing.

CHANGE A LIFE DIRECTION

For over thirty years, The Center • A Place of HOPE has been helping people change their lives for good. We treat depression, anxiety, eating disorders, trauma, PTSD, addiction, and OCD.

We believe in a whole-person approach to treatment that integrates all aspects of a person's life, including:

- Emotional well-being
- Physical health
- Spiritual peace
- Relational happiness
- Intellectual growth
- Nutritional vitality

Let us help you reclaim, restore, and reconnect to a healthy life.

WWW.APLACEOFHOPE.COM

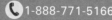 1-888-771-5166   ✉ info@aplaceofhope.com